Praise for *21*

"Daisey's hilarious, heartbreaking, and
life inside what may be the world's stra
One of the best books ever written abou................

—Jon Katz, *Slashdot*

"Wonderful . . . [Daisey's] often vociferous malice is delicious."

—Bruce Weber, *The New York Times*

"Mike Daisey does what Michael Moore once did for General Motors."

—*Entertainment Weekly*

"You'll LOL (laugh out loud)."

—Kerry Hannon, *USA Today*

"A brilliant, honest, and side-splitting account of the strangest company the
world has ever seen. Mike Daisey is the tech world's answer to Tom Green,
Michael Moore, Spaulding Grey, Jean Shepherd, and Mark Twain."

—Bill Lessard, coauthor of *Netslaves:True Tales of
Working the Web*

"For those still nursing a new economy hangover, Mike Daisey's funny and
evocative memoir serves up the hair of the dog that bit them."

—Andy Borowitz, *New Yorker* and *New York Times*
humorist and author of *The Trillionaire Next Door*

"Imagine a memoir by a grunt worker at the Ford Motor Company circa
1910, or from Monsanto circa 1950. Then imagine that memoirist as neurotic and very funny. Mike Daisey has done us a service by revealing the
dorky, scary truth about Amazon.com before it's too late."

—Neal Pollack, author of *The Neal Pollack Anthology
of American Literature*

"*21 Dog Years* is more than just one man's adventures in Webland. It's a
farce, a confessional, and a love story; laugh-out-loud funny and surprisingly
poignant."

—Robert Spector, author of *Amazon.com: Get Big Fast*

Mike Daisey

Free Press
New York London Toronto Sydney Singapore

21 Dog Years

A Cube Dweller's Tale

FREE PRESS

A Division of Simon & Schuster, Inc.

1230 Avenue of the Americas

New York, NY 10020

First Free Press paperback edition 2003

FREE PRESS and colophon are trademarks of Simon & Schuster, Inc.

For information about special discounts for bulk purchases,
please contact Simon & Schuster Special Sales:
1-800-456-6798 or business@simonandschuster.com

Designed by Bonni Leon Berman
Calligraphy by John Stevens

Manufactured in the United States of America

10   9   8   7   6   5   4   3   2   1

The Library of Congress has cataloged the hardcover edition as follows:
Daisey, Mike, date.
    21 dog years : doing time @ Amazon.com / Mike Daisey.
      p. cm.
    1. Amazon.com—History. 2. Internet bookstores—United States—
History—20th century. 3. Electronic commerce—United States—
History—20th century. 4. Daisey, Mike—Amazon.com—Biography.
I. Title: Twenty-one dog years : doing time @ Amazon.com. II. Title:
Doing time @ Amazon.com. III. Title.
Z473.A485 D35 2002
380.1'45002'028454678—dc21   2002025526

ISBN 0-7432-2580-5
    0-7432-3815-X (Pbk)

Contents

For Jean-Michele

It is difficult not to marvel at the imagination which was implicit in this gargantuan insanity. If there must be madness something may be said for having it on a heroic scale.

—John Kenneth Galbraith, *The Great Crash*

It was one of those rare smiles with a quality of eternal reassurance in it, that you may come across four or five times in life. It faced—or seemed to face—the whole external world for an instant, and then concentrated on *you* with such an irresistible prejudice in your favor. It understood you just so far as you wanted to be understood, believed in you as you would like to believe in yourself and assured you that it had precisely the impression of you that, at your best, you hoped to convey. Precisely at that point it vanished.

—F. Scott Fitzgerald, *The Great Gatsby*

1

Dilettante

When Amazon went to temping companies to recruit future employees, it gave a simple directive: send us your freaks. I know this is true because the people at the temping companies, not the sharpest knives in the drawer, would tell the people they were recruiting that this was the requirement. Not that it stopped me, no sir. I might not precisely regard myself as a professional freak, but as job descriptions go it falls well within my range.

I am a dilettante. I do many things, but none particularly well. It is the art of not applying yourself, the only craft I have studied my entire life. Like so many others of my generation, I cherish the delusion that I have superpowers buried deep inside me. They're awaiting the perfect trigger—radiation, a child in danger—and in that defining moment I will finally know my birthright: mutant healing factor, terrifying strength, maybe kick-ass retractable admantium claws. In a good daydream, it's all three.

When you know that you are destined for greatness by virtue of your mutant heritage it is difficult to apply yourself to normal life. Why waste the effort when you know that your potential is so tremendous? Better to wait. Better not to try, to save yourself for the Great Works to come. Nothing you do will ever be more than a footnote in light of your own unimaginable future, so save your breath and bide your time. Nurture your talent. Read a book. Play Nintendo.

It's a depressing life. The word dilettante derives from the Italian *dilettare,* meaning to delight in. Well, no one buys that—not even the dilettantes. It's a tough racket that favors the young: I was twenty-five and rapidly becoming the only practicing dilettante left from my college class. Being a dilettante is the opposite of having a viable career, and most people discover they don't enjoy starving, so they find a life and quickly settle into their private hells by choice or inertia.

I do have an advantage in the dilettante market; I have a bachelor's degree in aesthetics. No, really. At interviews it's the first thing people ask about, and I can tell they want to laugh at me. I think they should—it would be a great release for everyone involved. I should have known something was wrong when the recruiting professional for Amazon said my degree was the reason she had called.

Majoring in aesthetics seemed like a good idea at the time—

something that would free me up for the life of a wandering scholar without earthly ties, a book-oriented Caine from *Kung Fu*. You see, I'd grown up in far northern Maine, in the small town of Fort Kent, at the absolute end of U.S. Route 1. There's actually a sign where the road ends, next to the bridge to Canada: HERE ENDS U.S. ROUTE 1, WHICH BEGINS IN KEY WEST, FLORIDA.

This pronouncement contradicted the idea we were fed in school that roads had no end. Its presence reinforced something that I had always known, even as a child. Growing up between the paper mill and the potato field, it was clear to me that there were places out of which you could not maneuver, places with ends so dead that they defied inhabitants to imagine another way of life. In my eyes that sign had always read: HERE IS THE END OF THE ROAD, AND HERE IS WHERE YOU MUST STAY.

Bragging about how "rural" your upbringing was is like comparing penises—someone else's tin shack is always further up the mountain. But I usually win, owing to a unique topological irregularity: no matter where you are, Fort Kent is far, far away. These anecdotes sketch some of northern Maine's character:

a) During winter, gasoline turns to jelly in your tank if you leave your car unheated overnight, so everyone puts a bare light bulb under the hood. My mother goes a step further and puts blankets on the hood, tucking the car in like a baby.

b) My sister and I would get very excited when the family drove to Presque Isle, a town about two hours south, because they had a traffic light. We would chant, "Traffic light traffic light traffic light!" This behavior persisted through adolescence.

c) I spent one half of my waking hours in the winter months (of which there were nine) cutting, lifting, stacking, and throwing wood. I was a dilettante even then: I was not good at cutting, lifting, stacking, or throwing, but I had a passing familiarity with all the wood-heating arts.

When I went off to my hoity-toity microivy college I discovered that all I wanted in life was to dissolve into a mist of intellectualism that would creep around the hills and vales of New England. I would be a professional letter writer. I would be a freelance intellectual. I would study Etruscan vases here, equestrian history there, and simply float about the academic world, never again settling in one place or doing anything real like holding a job or, God forbid, lifting another piece of wood.

By naming my course of independent study "aesthetics" I could take a lot of courses that intrigued me, like acting and writing, ignore the ones I felt would waste my time, and generally subvert the entire point of the well-rounded liberal arts education for which I had taken out huge student loans. *Ah, youth! Was there nothing I could not accomplish? A young man escapes his fate in the bleak frozen wastes of Maine to become* . . . I had no idea. All I felt was a vague sense of grand entitlement and a fervent desire never to work an honest day in my life.

In some ways it was the curse of talent; there was a whole list of things in which I showed great promise. But there is a hell of a gap between "talented" and "successful," and to bridge it you need something called "will." My teachers begged me to dedicate myself—just a little—and said I would really blossom. I dug in my heels and refused. I feigned scorn and indignation but really I was just too scared to apply myself. I was afraid I would discover my limitations. Better not to know. Better to be free and easy and cultivate an air of smug accomplishment. Nurture my talent. Read another book. Play some more Nintendo.

But I miscalculated. I failed to go to graduate school, and it is difficult to be a wandering scholar without scholarship. So I went to Seattle and became disaffected, instantly. It was automatic in the nineties—if you entered the Seattle city limits and were a white liberal arts graduate with an uncertain future, you automatically became shiftless, distrustful of authority, and disaffected.

We are talking about slackers, an unavoidable element in the cultural landscape of the nineties. Rather than work in fields that grant traditional rewards (money, homes, cars), slackers took up eclectic pursuits (horror-movie collecting, fan-website building, coffee drinking). A true slacker had so many part-time projects, half-baked ideas, and hazy social initiatives that he was too busy to work a forty-hour week. This was not pedestrian laziness or sloth: professional slacking was an art.

Really, though, it was a newer version of tuning in, turning on, and dropping out brought on by economic malaise and social boredom. Boomers ruled everything: they were our parents, our teachers, our landlords, and the gatekeepers to every social or business institution. They talked about *Platoon*, remembered how great and terrible the sixties were, and refused to yield even a sliver of influence—you could either be a preteen and get marketed to, or you could be thirtysomething. No wonder a popular response among my peers was to *check out*.

Seattle was ground zero for slackers. The swift rise and fall of the grunge movement brought a wave of glam and celebrity to an otherwise sleepy city, and even after Kurt Cobain blew his head off at the height of his career it was allowed to keep its indie cred. Seattle had always been a boomtown, from the gold rush to Nirvana—the only question was what the next big thing would be.

For now an aura of grunge persisted. The city bulged with rockabilly singers, nouveau artists, and, of course, slackers. Across America the word was out that Seattle was this cool place full of relaxed people who really "got it," a great spot to be if you liked your arts intimate, your pace medium, didn't mind gray skies, and weren't concerned about getting ahead. It doesn't take a rocket scientist to see how slacking would evolve into an art form there.

Something else was evolving in Seattle too—in a garage, the birthplace of every great and not-so-great grunge band. Amazon was building its first desks from doors.

So Amazon and I started in Seattle at about the same time.

➤ I didn't have the faintest idea what to do with my life, but no one else seemed to have a plan either, which was comforting. I chose to immerse myself in the scene, writing fitfully and acting in fringe theater. One night, I was standing onstage in an unheated garage performing Jean Genet's *The Balcony* as the Bishop, wearing full Catholic regalia, a twelve-pound miter, and Greek *cothurni,* which are fifteen-inch platform heels. My giant robes were open and I was naked and about to masturbate while delivering a speech about sinning. I had expressed some reservations about this particular bit of business, but the director had told me that it would be "decadently fabulous," and although I meant to refuse in shock and horror, I had somehow never gotten around to it.

Anyway, there I was, exposed, about to begin the speech, when a family walked in. Mother, father, two little girls—late arrivals. I'll never know why they thought Genet would make a good family show. One of the little girls, not three feet from my naked Bishopness, stared wide-eyed with horror, but I honestly think I was more scared than she was. And it was at that very moment that I thought of Boylan, my fiction professor in school, telling me: "Daisey, you shouldn't go to grad school yet. Get out in the real world. You need to do a real job or you'll have nothing to work with."

So I took a deep breath and did my real job.

> ### ➤ Exposing myself to minors

didn't pay especially well, so I was making the rent by temping, a popular slacker occupation. It all runs together: *Seattle, disaffected, temping,* like a professional diagnosis, a syndrome. *Doctor, Doctor, what's wrong with him? Why is he so jaded, so cynical, and so goddamn poor?* The doctor shines a light, cops a quick feel while making the subject cough, speaks into his microrecorder: *Seattle. Disaffected. Temping. Treatment: regular doses of dogma to encourage development of a belief system. Subject is delaying adulthood and responsibility by pretending he is possessed by an unknowable destiny, chosen by fate, et cetera. Subject's head is currently located very far inside subject's ass.*

I really enjoyed temping; it agreed with me. I was living in a room over a crack den for two hundred dollars a month, which meant I could afford to take months off between assignments and simply drift, directionless and guilt-free. I often had to step over the passed-out junkie who lived across the hall, but I was in love with the way I didn't obey the corporate clock—at 10:00 A.M. on a Tuesday or 2:00 P.M. on a Thursday you would find me asleep. Sleep! Who knew I had been so starved for it? It was heaven.

The idea of being a permanent employee terrified and perplexed me—those who were looked uniformly unhappy and if you asked them, they would say that yes, indeed, they were miserable. It was hard to imagine how I could or would ever enter their world, even though more and more of my friends were emigrating to that great undiscovered country of medical insurance and 401 (k) plans.

Not so for me—I knew my place. I saw myself as a mercenary of the temping world. It was an ongoing fetish fantasy in which the good folks at Parker Staffing Services were sergeants, barking orders:

"Listen up, you weak-kneed vomit-licking dogs! Hamilton and Fitch needs a receptionist on the forty-second floor. It's lawyers—it'll be ugly. Who wants it?"

"Sir! I am trained for all reception duties, including simpering and fawning!"

"Daisey. Brave words. You want to live forever?"

"No, sir! I can also kill a man in three ways with a pencil, sir!"

"You like nine dollars an hour?"

"I like it fine, sir! Whatever it takes to serve those fucking lawyers, sir!"

"Goddamn right. Get on over there, Daisey. Move it!"

I loved the illusion of freedom: *this job is terrible, but at least I don't have to stay like the rest of these poor bastards.* This is the linchpin on which temping turns, the idea that you are free to walk at any time. It is an illusion: I never left an assignment early, never really made use of the "flexibility" I had in my grasp. The temping companies encourage you to think of yourself as a "temporary staffing professional" and work at instilling pride and polish into their recruits. Before long you are loyal to the temping company and unwilling to end a contract early.

When Parker called me because I had the gall to request and then take two days off, I was told by my liaison: "At Parker we insist that temping be your first priority."

"That's odd."

"Why?"

"Does anybody make temping their first priority? I mean, are you really flooded with folks who went to college dreaming of the day they would be temps, fiercely loyal to whatever employer wanted them on that one particular day?"

Silence.

"You know what I'm getting at, don't you?"

Silence.

"I'm pretty certain you didn't dream, all those years ago over the keg at Beta Phi Epsilon, that you would arrive at this lofty height, a placement officer discussing the ethics of temp work with an aesthetics major. We are not so different, you and I, are we?"

Silence.

"I guess this means that I can't have this Friday off?"

"You can have every Friday off."

"Oh? Oh. I see."

After being expelled from my agency I became very apathetic about the temping industry. I was indignant that I had been let go so abruptly; I felt betrayed, after the years I had spent in loyalish service. I found myself thinking, *What do they think I am, their slave?* That the question was rhetorical hadn't dawned on me. Only teenagers, dogs, and dilettantes are capable of this flavor of thinking.

It was summer and so I whiled away the time in a variety of exciting action poses: reading, sleeping, watching television, and a variant form of the reading pose that incorporated eating. My girlfriend and I became obsessed with *The Newlywed Game,* hosted by the creepy Bob Eubanks. A trained viewer can predict which couple will win within minutes of the show's opening—the couple with the largest smiles who strike each other while still smiling always wins, just like in real life. We played Super Mario Kart obsessively. We bought a Rocket Chef after the television told us to do that—it was always telling us to do all sorts of things in those days.

I was feeling very Zen and willing to listen to the advice of inanimate objects because I wanted nothing—I was in love. Jean-Michele had just become my live-in girlfriend, and it was the first time I had ever moved in with someone. I left my artistically hip neighborhood for a much more sedate burb that cost a lot more than the crack den, but I didn't care. We were delirious in love—we spent all day having sex and fighting, both at the same time when we could manage it.

Cross Anaïs Nin with Encyclopedia Brown and you get Jean-Michele—sensual, funny, and possessed by the dark, passionate practicality of the Polish. I learned about Poland quickly: the first time I met her family we sat in the garden drinking and getting to know one another, two activities that are indistinguishable and interchangeable to the Poles.

We were all drunk and laughing when Babcia came up from downstairs. *Babcia* is Polish for *grandmother* but with Babcia it had become a capital *B:* she was the Babcia of Babcias, the woman about whom I had heard a hundred stories, who had delivered her family from the horrors of the Nazi occupation and to America.

Jean-Michele loves her more than life itself, and meeting her for the first time I was amazed at how tiny she was: I was certain I could fit this matriarch inside of my thigh, that I could have smuggled her over the East German border if necessary. Later I would learn that she was also capable of feeding a person so insistently that they could actually die of a cream-induced embolism right at the kitchen table.

My first glimpse of Babcia was not over a bowl of borscht—she had come outside to find out why we were laughing and shouting at the tops of our lungs. Her eyes were bright and disapproving as she surveyed all of us committing the cardinal sin of drinking in the garden. *Think of the neighbors!* and *Be quiet and careful!* were artfully knitted into the shawls she gave away at Christmas. Babcia remains the only woman I have ever met who can actually make guilt shimmer like heat waves in summer.

Maybe she was equally unhappy with all of us, but her gaze settled on me—I had obviously brought this laughing into the house. I saw how clearly I was read, judged, and found unworthy. She knew what I did for a living (nothing) and my ambitions (AWOL). Under duress I would have admitted to being a slacker, but beneath her withering gaze I felt I had earned a more emasculating title: bum. Man without job. Dead weight.

She stood for a minute until everyone else noticed her, and when she had the attention of everyone she said in a clear voice: "You're all laughing now, but you'll be crying later." Then she walked back inside the house without another word.

➡ Later that night I stared at the ceiling with Jean-Michele curled beside me, and for the first time I knew with certainty that these days weren't going to last. I had no idea what Babcia had meant with her factually accurate, yet depressingly Polish pronouncement. Her melodrama had struck a nerve. Mystical Nazi-escaping grandmothers are not to be trifled with.

The lazy indulgences would have to go. I wasn't playing "find yourself" as my parents had, or fighting a war, or even learning tai chi. I needed to pull my own weight, get things moving, and acquire some direction. So I would find a job. Not more temping, a Real Job™. In the morning, first thing.

I did nothing the next day. Or the next. Rinse, repeat. Every night in bed I would tally the reasons I had to work, think of how we could not afford to live like this, watching the bank account dip and dry up. Rinse, repeat. You can lead a horse to water but that doesn't mean he'll go to the office. Rinse, repeat.

My perversity saved me—more specifically my obsession with tooth decay. There was little wrong with my teeth, but I reasoned it was only a matter of time. One of my foremost neuroses is the condition of my teeth. They have tiny cavities, and I'm always afraid that these tiny cavities will become Huge Cavities, which will in turn offer easy access to a Tooth Infection, which will expand into a Gum Infection and then a Jaw Infection, which will finally climb up into my head and become a Brain Infection. Then my brain will swell up inside my skull and I will die, a condition I saw once on *St. Elsewhere.*

I knew that this was both true and possible because my mother, bless her black heart, had sent me a newspaper article on the phenomenon, which I read and then attached to the fridge with magnets. Once it's on the fridge it is more real than real: it is fact.

This meant that it was time to get real health insurance, and real health insurance meant getting a Real Job™. Jean-Michele liked the idea. She thought employment would make me more attractive—not only to Babcia but to her. It was like a wake-up call from God. Faced with the prospect of losing my girlfriend and dying like a toothless bear of some third world–style gum infection, I was now on a serious job hunt.

My first call was prompted by an ad in the *Seattle Weekly* under the nondescript heading: CUSTOMER SERVICE TIER 1: LAME TITLE—COOL JOB. The rest of the ad mentioned good pay, flexible hours, and a "hip and quirky work environment." I faxed them my SAT scores and my transcripts, which was odd for an office job—no one had ever cared about my academic background before. I was thrilled when they called me five minutes later.

When I needed a Real Job™, there, like my white knight, was Amazon.com.

2

Freak Parade

What I didn't know, and what Amazon wasn't telling, was that they were fishing for a very particular kind of worker for their customer service department. After all, the net was everywhere, so location would no longer be a factor, and every website basically looked the same, give or take a few design widgets and Flash-animated dancing monkeys. So to win you would have to provide the world's greatest shopping experience, and to get that you would need smart, intelligent, motivated people who wanted to perform the mind-numbing routine of telephone customer service.

Normally it would be a Herculean task to find bright, college-educated people willing to work in customer service farms for a starting salary equal to that at the local Taco Bell. But these were not normal times. By 1998, fairy tales of boundless riches and glorious stock options were percolating through the media like a morphine drip, and Seattle was awash in disaffected intellectuals. Easy meat.

To catch their prey Amazon was anxious to prove that it was no ordinary company. That's why SAT scores were requested, GREs if you had them, please, your college and high school transcripts as well as a written examination made up of book report–style questions about literature and grammar tests. It created an air of exclusivity: you felt as though you'd beaten out hundreds for this rare and special chance to work for nine dollars an hour answering the phone.

My first meeting with the recruiter was a revelation. She was a polite and talkative lady with thick glasses and an overbite. Her favorite maneuver was to breathe in through her mouth, flare her nostrils, and then blast the air back out her nose—a human air conditioner.

She had called me on the phone right away, she told me, because of my background.

"My background?"

"Your degree."

"Oh. I'm sorry about that—" I began, preparing to launch into my standard corporate apology for not having a background in human resources or political science and why I was still employable, please, give me a chance, I won't let you down.

"I think you are exactly what we are looking for."

That stopped me dead. No one had ever said that. I thought for a moment about what this job was: customer service. Selling books over the Internet. Unless there was a hidden element of art criticism to the job I really couldn't see how aesthetics applied.

"Oh," I said.

"Yes, we have placed a large number of Ph.D.s and M.A.s at Amazon. It's a very literate group, very cutting-edge. Young. I think that with your background you'd fit right in."

"Oh."

"Amazon is about broadening horizons, interfacing with technology, and taking a can-do approach to corporate solutions."

"I like technology . . . I like horizons." Jesus, I was giving a terrible interview. I was normally very good in interviews, better at them than at actually doing work, but I still couldn't believe this woman actually thought I was qualified to do something. No one should believe that. It was throwing me off.

"Great! You know, Amazon is a very *diverse* workplace." She put particular emphasis on diverse, as though it were a proper noun. "A lot of people with noserings, purple hair and tattoos, things like that . . . you know?" She verbally nudged me with her elbow. "You know?"

"Oh yeah. Yeah. That's part of why I'm . . . ah . . . interested." *They have purple hair?*

"Excellent! You know," she said conspiratorially, "Amazon is always telling us to find them the freaks. They want the freaks, you know, people who might not fit in elsewhere. So when I saw your résumé . . . ah . . ." She lost track of her tact for a moment. "Ah . . . I thought you would really find a home here. People need a home to work in, you know?"

"Well, I agree with that."

She nodded vigorously. I nodded as well. She nodded back at me. We both sat there, nodding at each other like a couple of windup toys working through our hiring script. I was nodding to say: *Yes, please give me a job.* Her nodding said: *Yes, you are a freak.* We nodded all the way to signing me up for an informational meeting about the company and the job.

Years later I found out that the staffing company had a bin for the Amazon applications separate from all other assignments. The receptionist saw that the bin was labeled F.P. and asked what it stood for. "Oh, that's for Freak Parade," she was told. "You know, the Amazonians."

→ The informational session for prospective Amazon recruits was what really convinced me to join the company. It was held in a fantastic conference room at the top of one of Seattle's skyscrapers with floor-to-ceiling windows framing the Olympic Mountains, the Space Needle, and Puget Sound sparkling and glinting below. It was a postcard. I wouldn't have been surprised if I'd seen the Eiffel Tower and the Pyramids from those lofty heights, or if Amazon had gone to the trouble of having them digitally inserted.

And my God, those people! The four Amazonians who came to speak with us had the clearest, cleanest skin that I'd ever seen. Two men, two women—they said they worked in customer service, which they referred to as "CS." Two of the four wore REI fleece vests, and all four had some slight variation of the same khaki Dockers pants. And that hygiene. *These folks must have an amazing medical plan that includes plastic surgery or genetic reprogramming,* I thought. I was encouraged in my quest to prevent tooth decay.

I would never see those people again in my entire time at Amazon. I assume they worked for a black-ops section that specialized in providing fake employees who are startlingly sharp, attractive, and painfully fit.

We settled back and they began to talk about Linux tools and server uptime, and I suddenly realized that these people were geeks. Serious computer geeks who looked and smelled great.

"Amazon's back end database is compiled nightly . . ."

"Yeah, we play hard and we work hard."

"Website builds are served from a main template . . ."

"Please wear whatever you are comfortable in and express yourself—Amazon is a free environment for your mind to play in. We work hard and we play hard."

"You'll be learning UNIX tools to work directly with the database, which is hard, but you know, you learn a lot and that's part of why it's great to work so hard."

"You need to be prepared to give a hundred and ten percent here . . . but we play hard, too."

There was a certain inescapable sameness to their responses. They seemed fixated on the words *working, playing,* and *Jeff. Jeff* came up constantly. I had no idea who Jeff was.

"Jeff's great. He works hard and plays hard, and he's around all the time."

"Jeff's got an unforgettable laugh. It's really . . . wow, I mean, it is really *him,* you know? It is really *Jeff.*"

"Jeff built this company out of nothing, really just himself and a few guys in a garage and now . . . all of *this.*"

Ah, Jeff must be the founder.

I really wasn't clued in to what was going on, but from the way the sexy tech workers talked about Amazon.com, it appeared I'd really missed the boat. Contextually I picked up the first rule of many I would learn during my time at Amazon: *The illusion that something has momentum and drive is as valuable as having momentum and drive.* This led to an instant corollary: *You can create something from nothing, if you spin it correctly.*

To give you an idea of how clueless I was, I had originally assumed that Amazon.com was a lesbian Internet bookstore, owing to the historical origins of the word *Amazon* along with the company's reputation for being "progressive." Luckily, the geeks set me straight early in the presentation:

"AMAZON.COM IS CALLED AMAZON.COM BE-CAUSE THE AMAZON IS THE EARTH'S LARGEST RIVER, AND WE ARE THE EARTH'S LARGEST STORE. OUR GOAL IS TO PROVIDE THE MOST CUSTOMER-CENTRIC EXPERIENCE IN HISTORY FOR THIS ENTIRE PLANET." I don't know how management types at Amazon succeed in speaking in capital letters and in boldface, but they do.

I was enchanted. These tech-savvy, attractive, and well-spoken workers appeared blissfully happy. They were everything the folks I had worked with at all my temping assignments were not; they had everything my actor friends lacked in their work-a-day drudgery.

I had always had a love affair with geekdom but it sadly wasn't reciprocal. I loved geek talk and did geek things but lacked some essential introvertedness that would allow me to really be one of their kind. My friend John diagnosed me during a heated discussion about George Lucas's decision to allow Greedo to shoot first in the Cantina scene on the remixed DVD version of *Star Wars:* "Michael, your problem is your geekness lacks conviction. You do not bear the Mark of Kirk." When I asked John what the Mark of Kirk was, he snorted derisively and I lost another ten points.

These Amazon folk weren't supermodels, but they were embodiments of a kind of higher geek ideal: people who could make a UNIX box dance from the command line, look great while doing it, and then go dancing at a rave. The opportunity to be near them, surrounded by their coolness and learning from them while being paid, sounded like heaven itself. If I couldn't be a geek, at least I could be in their company.

And what company! Though I hadn't known who they were until that day, I was convinced they were making history. That phrase came into my head right from the beginning, and I'm certain they placed it there. I had a vague sense of riches, of future glory. No one spoke in specifics—they did say that there were stock options, which sounded glamorous compared to hourly wages. For all the sound and fury we left the meeting knowing about the same amount as when we walked in . . . but I was now filled with a lust I had never experienced for *working at a job*.

I took the elevator back down to earth full of hope, and the first thing I saw while waiting for the bus was the cover of the *Seattle Weekly,* featuring a one word splash: AMAZON.CULT.

The article caused quite a stir locally. It was a rather straightforward story: someone had joined Amazon in the very same position for which I was now jockeying, experienced a lot of weird stuff, and fled.

The details of the weirdness were striking. The author said that the employees were aggressively cheerful, dogmatic, and obsessive. He said that Amazon took micromanagement to a new level, that the corporate culture demanded unwavering loyalty, puritan devotion, and a zeal that could not be justified by the pay or the experience. Finally, he revealed that he had left Amazon and ended up with a contracting position at Microsoft, which I now believe must be like trading the third circle of hell for the sixth—different tortures, different bosses, same consequences.

Now, this is just a piece of advice I offer for free: if you should ever be in a position where you're going to join a company but haven't yet signed any papers, and if a major newspaper publishes a feature about how the company you are about to go to work for is a cult . . . say no. Thank you, no, it's all right. Sorry to have wasted your time.

There are jobs out there that don't require you to drink the Kool-Aid. Even if you are desperate, signs like these should give you pause. And I was far from desperate; I was a well-educated white man with a shiftless streak. By all accounts, I should never have gone back for the training—everything in my character would seem to rebel against it. It should have. It really should.

I told Jean-Michele about it over coffee at the Allegro, one of Seattle's ubiquitous coffee houses. It is a conversation I cannot forget because so much was unsaid, and as I talked and talked I could hear a peculiar timbre creeping into my voice, foreign zeal and enthusiasm taking root between my verbs and adjectives.

"It was great. They're good-looking, and the people are sharp, and sales are growing end to end in a paradigm of growth. . . . It's a very explosive net business." I had only a tenuous grasp of what I was talking about.

"Hmm." She seemed unimpressed. "Why did they want your SAT scores?"

"Uh, to . . . you know, quality control."

"I don't know anybody who does that." She stared at me over her latte. She has a killer stare that can rattle me, but this time I sailed through it.

"Oh, that just speaks to the, ah, the *quality* people they want for this."

"Hmm."

"Why do you ask?"

"I don't know." She did know. She wasn't saying. I took the initiative.

"They're a customer-centric company. We want to be the most customer-centric company in the world, and you need really intelligent, sharp people to pull that off."

"We?"

"They. I mean they. But I'm hoping it will be we."

"I thought you were just going to do this until you heard back on the editing position?" I had some leads on an editorial assistant job.

"Yeah, I'm still doing that. I just mean that while I'm here I want to, you know, fit in. Anything worth doing is worth doing well, you know."

She stirred her latte. *Anything worth doing is worth doing well.* How unlike Michael to say that, she must have thought. It was a summer evening in Seattle and night was falling. We were in the upstairs section, which was open air. Warm night. Beyond her I could see the colors changing behind the University of Washington, where Jean-Michele was studying theater.

"Did you read the article?" she asked me neutrally.

"In the *Weekly*?"

"Yes."

"The one about Amazon?"

"Yes."

"Yes, I did read that. Yes."

We sat in silence as it got darker. She wouldn't ask more; she was happy enough that I might be working, and with enthusiasm—that was more than she'd dared wish for.

In the weeks ahead I would vilify the article's author, explain that he had never been an Amazonian—why, he hadn't even made it through training! A sissy! He exaggerated, I said. He was cold and ironic and didn't *get* Amazon. As if Amazon were an infection you could catch. As if.

But in that moment we were quiet. There was no anger or disagreement, only a simple, unspoken question: *What are you thinking, Michael? Tell me.* I said nothing to that. You can't tell someone what you don't know yourself.

Freak Parade

3

Doors for Desks

When I was first born into the corporate workforce I became possessed with an insatiable lust to steal office supplies. What childhood indulgences led to this I do not know—too many Crayolas, a penchant for eating paste—but the compulsion reared its head when I started temping. I also discovered I was not alone.

Let's be clear—everybody filches *some* supplies. When you are a cube jockey it's the safest form of rebellion. I'd find myself acting out passive-aggressive impulses by bringing home pieces of my workplaces and depriving my enemies of the same.

Well, Mr. Hotpants Lawyer thinks he is going to yell at me because his focaccia is dry? Oh, he's got a world of hurt coming—I am so going to open a can of whupass on this sorry sonofabitch, a can of whupass I like to call, "I Ain't Got No Dry-Erase Pens." I know he doesn't have them, because I've got every last one here in my backpack. I'm rich! Shit, I might just give them to friends, let neighbor kids have some, hand them to unemployed folks on the street who look like they might want to write and then erase something. If Mr. Lawyer Man thinks he can tangle with me, he's going to wake up without his legal pads. Won't be much of a law office without legal pads, will it? Oh, they laughed at me when I said a temp could rule the world— now, look at the heights from which I mock you all and know despair! Despair! I will bury you! I will bury you! It's at this point in the fantasy that I take off my shoe and bang it on the table until they take me away.

I think everyone probably steals a little more than they intend to because, in an office world where everything is regulated, every gesture of freedom is prized above rubies. The more you take, the more you know you've gotten away with. It's easy to see how someone with certain flaws in their character might become trapped in a cycle of addiction—the futility of their pointless, deskbound existence writ starkly in the inventory of pointless, extravagant items stolen. I've discovered over the years that I am hardly alone. In small, embarrassed voices many have told me how they, too, find some comfort in their collections of Post-its and Wite-Out.

A partial inventory of my filched office supplies:

67 legal pads, yellow
62 transparent page protectors
31 lined pads, 8 1/2" by 11", white
15 spiral-bound notebooks, white
8 rulers: 5 plastic, 2 wooden, 1 drafting
5 staplers: 3 full-size, 2 miniature
4 staple removers
4 mousepads: 2 Amazon-branded, 1 blue, 1 black
3 boxes black felt-tip pens, 0.5 mm (15 count)
3 bottles Wite-Out
2 gel wrist protectors
2 boxes black felt-tip pens, 0.7 mm (15 count)
2 boxes black Sharpies (20 count)
1 box red Sharpies (20 count)
1 box green Sharpies (20 count)
2 packages Post-its, pink, medium
2 packages Post-its, yellow, medium
1 package Post-its, yellow, large

There are also some odder items that defy logical explanation—the printer cartridge to an ink-jet printer I do not own and the whiteboard markers for whiteboards I will never have. This pirate booty fills up a cheap IKEA cabinet in the corner of our small apartment. Sometimes I like to open the cabinet and rearrange my loot, marveling at its quantity, smelling the markers until I am dizzy with possibility. I imagine this is how dragons in bad fantasy novels feel.

Jean-Michele's Polish sensibilities make her disdainful of such waste, and she is both repulsed and aroused by my ability to simply *take without cause*. She insists on revisiting the subject every few months.

"So . . . you just walk out with this stuff."

"Yes."

"No one ever says anything?"

"Nope."

"I would never do that. I would be scared to death."

I feel a surge of pride in my desperadoness. It's nice to have your mate admire you, even if she knows you are an idiot.

"What would you do if they caught you?"

"That's a good question." Pause. "I'm not sure that's possible."

"Of course it's possible."

"It's like jaywalking. No enforcement."

"This is Seattle. They catch and prosecute jaywalkers here."

"True." Seattle is America's Most Polite City, which means that even if race relations go to hell and the homeless are corralled into a few square blocks while anarchists break all the Starbucks windows, police officers will still be available to enforce the jaywalking laws. God bless the Emerald City.

Near the end of my temping career Jean-Michele looked into my cabinet. "You keep taking bigger and bigger things," she said. "There has to be a point where they notice. I'm afraid I'm going to come home one night and you'll have a desk and rolling chair. Then you'll end up in jail and I won't be able to bail you out and then you'll be in prison and our future unborn children will have a criminal for a father—if you even get a chance to father them from jail—and we'll be forced to copulate in the conjugal visit trailer!"

"That really would be something."

"You're never going to use all this." She knew she was losing. "Just try to keep it all in this corner."

You can understand now that when I entered Amazon for training I had more than a passing interest in the location and quality of the office supplies. This, I have always felt, is the best way to divine the true nature of a workplace; it's the whitebread modern equivalent of haruscimancy, the Roman art of divination from bird entrails. As luck would have it, the supply area was adjacent to the training room where my first four weeks of Amazonian life would take place, so before stepping in for the first day I quickly scanned the contents.

In a word: schizophrenic. There were huge quantities of supplies in an open arrangement, which usually denotes abundance and largesse, but the pens were Bics and the pads were the low-quality, yellow lined paper ones with chunks of undissolved wood I remembered from grade school. No Sharpies. No staplers. I had never seen such an ascetic display. The setup was brutally efficient and lacked all pretense of fun—and it looked cheap as hell for a thriving corporation with global reach.

Where were the Palm Pilots for all of us, and the personal wireless devices, the cell phones with their soothing ice-blue glow and ergonomically designed contours so our hands would never tire? Or the clear rubber balls that pulsed light when you bounced them? I loved those. Dot-coms constantly gave them away on the streets to "raise awareness"—they were cool, but all they made me aware of was that I wanted more glowing rubber balls.

As I waited for the first day of training to begin I remember wondering why the supplies looked so familiar. It only came to me much later, too late to serve as a final warning. A few months earlier I had worked as a receptionist at the law offices of a public defense fund, and the paper and pen quality there had been the same: aggressively cheap and bottom-rung. Of course the supplies were the same. Both companies were non-profits, run with higher ideals than the making of simple dollars. I was walking into the Big Tent Revival of capitalism, and the devout need neither stickies nor Sharpies, nor anything as base as roller-tipped, liquid-bearing 0.5 millimeter ball point pens. I didn't know that, but I was about to find out.

➤ Customer service training at Amazon was a harrowing experience. It lasted four weeks and was intense both in terms of what you learned and in how you were taught to love. In many ways it resembled training for a religious vocation; in the end it becomes obvious either that you were born for the life or that you were never meant to be there and will never be heard from again.

At first glance it was utterly simple: we were going to be phone operators at a catalog company, like Sears, except the catalog would be a website and some of the service would be in the form of emails instead of phone calls. Since a lot of people had advanced degrees this should have been a cakewalk. The class was four weeks long only because Amazon needed to cull the weaker elements and make certain they were getting the troops they needed to win their war.

Our training class began with about thirty people. As it progressed individuals began to disappear—usually two or three a week. It was tacitly understood that anyone who didn't show up one day would not be coming back, but if you were gauche enough to ask the ever-perky trainers about the missing, they'd stiffen slightly as though they'd seen a wasp. You'd then get an assortment of eerily cheerful responses, always appropriately regretful:

"Jack is no longer with us."

"Jack has chosen to no longer be with us."

"Jack had to leave."

And this particularly creepy phrasing: "Jack elected to cease operations."

The trainers decided to address the whole Amazon.cult debacle right from the top. It went down like this: we're sitting in class, and the trainer comes to us and says, "Hello, I'm trainer Mandy, and I want talk to you about an article you may have read? The Amazon.cult article? Yes? Okay? I want to address any concerns that you might have about this? Does anyone have any concerns? Yes?"

Trainer Mandy has bright eyes, an impish smile, and the apparent inability to speak in anything other than rising intonations, making her patter sound like a stream of unanswerable questions. "Yes? You? What is your concern? Tell us?"

A straw-haired kid in an REI fleece: "Um . . . I was, I was . . . was . . . concerned that, uh, about that, the part where, uh, you said, it said you were *a cult*? It kinda freaked me out?" Apparently Mandy's disease was infectious.

She was Dramamine on an empty stomach. "OK, let's talk about those feelings? What do they mean by 'a cult'? Are they talking about our work ethic? What does that mean in their personal context? Their own point of view? The way we get things done?"

She made us feel better. She gave us the talk every day. Every single day. And so by the seventh or eighth day, when Mandy came out and said, "Today let's revisit the Amazon.cult—"

"No! Actually, that's cool, uh, Mandy, that's really, that's, uh, cool. Does anybody, any of you guys wanna—?"

"Fuck no."

"Nope."

"I'm good."

It was our first sign of consensus.

"We're all cool, Mandy. Let's just learn another UNIX tool or more about Jeff's vision or something. We're cool, we're really fine with it." And in our hearts, we were fine with it. Because we'd heard it over and over again and then made it part of ourselves. That's how corporate training works: whip, reward, repeat.

The trainers did mean well, that much you could be certain of. All day long they radiated goodwill, a palpable flow of bonhomie that threatened to drown everyone in the training room in which we were all locked together from eight to five.

And it was out of the goodness of their hearts that they shared with us a vision, a vision of what Amazon.com really was, and the part that we might play in its magnificent destiny. They did that by showing us training films like this one.

Imagine the American West as it appears in collectors' plates from the Franklin Mint, resplendent in grain, mountains, horses, buffalo, and barely sketched details. From the east, across the plains, come settlers, pacing relentlessly toward the camera à la Reservoir Dogs. *John Williams is playing, underscoring everything. This is Amazon.com, Earth's Most Customer-centric Company. More than just a dream, more than an idea, it is a religion, and like any good religion it has an origin myth of equal parts fear and awe. This is its story.*

The year is 1995. We begin with Jeff Bezos—geek savant, investment banker, and entrepreneur, like a latter-day Johnny Quest. You can see his face, determined and resolute, as he drives across America in a Toyota hatchback. His wife is at the wheel and he's composing their business plan. They don't know what it is they're going to sell. They don't know why they're going to sell it. They don't even know what city they're driving to—they've told the movers that they will call them from the road to let them know where to go. But they know they're going to do it on the Internet. They have seen the future and they are going to grab it by the horns.

Jeff Bezos has vision and he's got moxie, he's got stamina, he has very little hair, and he's rolling his way into Seattle, City on the Sea. His wife and he have taken an enormous risk, abandoning high-paying jobs to chase a dream of 400 percent annual growth, which is what the net was doing in those days. All he needs to change the world is a large garage in which he will build a lot of desks made out of doors—flat, cheap doors from Home Depot, thus showing with one sharp symbol that this new company values money, eschews comforts, and has a warm, friendly atmosphere in which the CEO helps the new people build their desks.

You can sell anything on Jeff's Internet: books, CDs, DVDs, lawn furniture, cat litter, used medical waste, elephant ivory, lunch meat, slaves, anything. Jeff will be there, plugged right into each and every consumer, giving personalized recommendations, and people will find that just what they wanted has been brought right to their door and they will love it.

Thank God for this—before Jeff we were all concerned about the future of commerce. Who knew what they were going to buy next? Who knew what book would go best with their veal? Amazon will be there to guide us, to tell us what our favorites were, are, and have always been, to keep us fed with fresh things.

The army of settlers, outfitted with wagons, babies, and Palm Pilots, hail Jeff. They say, "Yes, you've got a vision," and they have purple hair and piercings and MBAs and greed and hunger and want, and they all crowd into that one garage! No one can stop it from growing and growing until it boils over into the city of Seattle, then America, then the world.

Market analysts, stunned and staggered, kiss the hem of

Doors for Desks

Jeff's robe. The settlers build huge warehouses with back-hoes and bulldozers. CEOs of old-school companies are impaled on spikes beside the road where children from Yahoo!, DoubleClick, and iVillage laugh at them. The digital village celebrates.

Everyone gives thanks that they are selling things, that they are getting big fast and never forgetting their humble origins. "It's still Day One," Mao once said—actually that was Jeff Bezos, but it sounds like something Mao would have said about the egalitarian workplace Amazonians now call home, where bureaucracy vanishes and only the best come to work each day.

At night, the settlers huddle around their fires as crotchety old-timers recount stories of the old days to growing masses of eager newcomers. A man eerily reminiscent of Lorne Greene speaks: "We'd sit by the fire, every day after work, cookin' a pot of beans, just thankful for the hard, hard work we'd done, makin' history. Thankful for the stock options. Ah . . . the stock went up twenty-five points today. Why?" He grins. "Nobody knows why. It's a mystery, just like the stars above are a mystery. Just like Amazon.com is a mystery."

And if we look up into the digitally enhanced stars, we can see Jeff Bezos himself, as a great Prudential ad, appearing as a seven-hundred-foot-high, googly-eyed Jesus, telling us, "You know, it's more than that—it's our dream. If you dream hard, if you work hard, and if you believe hard, you can make anything happen. Everybody who works at Amazon knows that. It's what brings us back to work every day."

Now we can see the workers and owners of Amazon.com triumphant, standing on the bodies of their enemies. Drunk and magnificent, the employees chug microbrewed beers and drive SUVs recklessly across the prairie, hitting buffalo. These noble workers were brave enough to say, "Goddamn yeah,

we're gonna work hard" and "Goddamn yeah, get rich too!"
They put their hearts and souls on the line, and the world did
listen, and the markets did listen too. And the stock did rise
and rise and rise and Amazon had a bright future ahead of it
for at least the next twelve fiscal months.

You hear the sweeping power chords, watch the slow-
motion doves flying into the sky like a bad Hong Kong flick. As
we head off into the future it seems certain that Amazon.com
will be the single-most customer-intensive company in the his-
tory of the world. Amen and hallelujah, praise Jesus and God
and Shiva, and may the market forces bless and protect us in
infinite growth, all our charts running up and to the right in
infinite progression, amen.

Then the training film fades to black, the word END appears,
the lights come back on, and we blink in the brightness of the
new day.

➤ In retrospect it seems so foolish

—many will read this and wonder how grown men and
women could get so worked up over a website that sells books.
It seems impossible that we could have believed that it would
change the world, but the evidence was all around us: the television coverage, the magazine and newspaper articles our
trainers showed us in endless succession. Immersed day after
day in the language of success we became heated and insistent
to everyone who asked, letting people know that the digital
revolution was happening *right now.* Quick, get on board
before it's too late!

There was the Old World and the New World, and a war
was coming in which Amazon would play a vital role, van-
quishing bad, brick-and-mortar corporations. We began to

believe that by supporting Amazon.com we would be helping to crush chains and monopolies and faceless bureaucracies. We were hopelessly naïve.

Overwhelmingly white, pale, doughy, and directionless before arriving at Amazon.com, we now talked incessantly about what books we were reading, and in the process discovered that our new colleagues were very well read, well spoken, highly educated. There were anime lovers, film critics of obscure Japanese horror pictures, scholars of Middle English literature, botanists. Pick your flavor of obscurity. We didn't know it at the time because we were all too well read, but we had another common denominator: we all wanted desperately to believe in something.

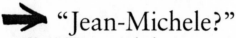 "Jean-Michele?"

"Yes?" We were in bed.

"I was wondering if you wanted to go to the Amazon picnic this weekend."

Jean-Michele cleared her throat, stalling for time. "Ah . . . you want to go to the Amazon company picnic?"

"It'll be really cool—they're going to have thirty different kegs, with a different microbrew in each one, and the Velcro wall thing, and Jeff will be in a dunking tank along with David Risher."

She counted out her points on her hands: "One, you never like to go to company picnics—no one does. Two, we're supposed to be performing at a fundraiser. Three—who the hell is David Risher?"

"He's a vice president of operations." As soon as I said it, I knew I was way out of my league.

"You want to meet a vice president?"

"Well, I wouldn't *mind*. I mean, he's a person, too—you shouldn't judge him so narrowly because of his success. Success is something we create."

"Michael, you aren't even *hired* yet. You're still a trainee."

"I know."

"You want to go to a picnic with a company that hasn't hired you?"

"Yes." My voice was small.

Jean-Michele sighed and turned on her side. I wonder what I sounded like, there in the dark making my small confession. "We can talk about it in the morning," she said. But we never did.

4

Geek Messiah

That I was actually able to believe in something created in me an uneasy mixture of pride and embarrassment. I think a lot of people my age feel similarly. We grew up immersed in irony—most of my life feels like someone else's movie unfurling scene by scene as I watch. I wanted to take control of the camera and finally do something that would matter. The degree in aesthetics probably didn't help, either.

All this detachment had made me hungry for the fruit of earnestness. I wanted to pick up an apple and know it was an apple and not some abstracted, twice-removed notion of an apple. I wanted an end to endless doubt and ironic equivocation. I wanted to feel as if I was entirely alive, making a difference, which is a blasphemy in the modern world—no one gets to be alive at their job. Looking back, I realize I would have been a perfect candidate for the Peace Corps, the Boy Scouts, or a fundamentalist branch of the Kiwanis Club if Amazon hadn't found me first.

I can't tell you how exciting, how stirring it was to be in the thick of something so deadly earnest, to be given permission to invest myself in a group. These people, my coworkers, were serious about Amazon, serious about our work, and everything was on the line. I'd never been in a group of hardworking people who all believed in the same thing—I had grown up Catholic. This was communism, but you got rich doing it, and that made it OK.

And that was the hook, you see: just as the disaffected intellectuals of ages past took their grievances and their angst to the Communist party, so now we took ours to capitalism. Whether you're talking Lenin or McDonald's the fever remains the same; if a leader can find the language needed to awaken people's zeal, he or she can receive blind devotion in return. You cannot buy that with money; although the lure of unrealized stock served as the spark for Amazon, it wasn't the essence. The essence was Jeff.

From beginning to end Amazon.com has always been a one-man operation. A one-Jeff operation. We may have been coached morning, noon, and night to believe that each and every one of us was equal, but the moment you met Jeff you realized that it simply wasn't true. He was a god, the still point around which the Amazonian world revolved—always has been, always will be, amen. Religions have their popes and prophets, and we had Jeff.

For a god, he was a plain guy. Of medium height and slight build, he resembled nothing so much as a bright and studious elf—Santa's second lieutenant. He had wispy brown hair, looked his thirtyish age, and was almost invariably dressed in a blue shirt, khaki pants, and nice shoes. In a sense it had become his uniform, and then by imitation the uniform of the dot-com movement.

Jeff's luminous brown eyes, huge and dewy, can hardly be confined to his face. They gesture. They leap out. They beckon. It is not an act—he is brilliant, deeply charismatic, and totally genuine. He is gentle, a rare trait in humans, particularly CEOs. You would trust him with your children; when you got home he would have taught them how to sequence DNA and how the kitchen sink disposal *really* works. I have never had a kinder or more human employer before or since— Jeff is amazingly dedicated to connecting with everyone in his company.

Workers at Amazon passed tantalizing details about Jeff back and forth like trading cards:

- Jeff grew up in Cuba and escaped to America as a young man. (False)
- Jeff repaired windmills as a teenager. (True)
- Jeff spent some of his childhood in a bubble due to an autoimmune deficiency. (False)
- Jeff used to brand, vaccinate, and castrate cattle. (True)
- Jeff started his own school for gifted middle-school children while in high school. (True)
- Jeff trained himself to have photographic recall. (False)
- Jeff loves *The Lord of the Rings* and *Dune*. (True)

- Jeff is worth billions but rents an apartment and drives a Toyota hatchback. (True)
- Jeff worked in investment banking before starting Amazon.com. (True)
- Jeff only sleeps three hours a night. (False)
- Jeff still responds to email at his public address: jeff@amazon.com. (True)

The last fact is the one that made the greatest impression on me early in my training. It tasted so wonderful in my mouth, like when as a child I thought that Santa hung out at the Pole all day reading our letters and taking notes. I asked a coworker about the email thing in the break room between sessions.

"Hey, msmith." His surname was Smith, but shortly after arriving at Amazon we started referring to everyone by their login—the abbreviated version of their name used to log into the network. I was mdaisey, he was msmith. Pronounced *em-smith*. Some names worked, some names didn't, but it could be addictive—if you started doing it for some you found yourself doing it for lots of people. It totally took over my speech patterns.

"Yeah?"

"We can write to Jeff at jeff@amazon.com. . . . Did you hear about that?"

"Yeah. Weird."

"Do you think he writes back?"

"I wouldn't if I were him but . . . yeah, I bet he does."

"Yeah, I bet he does too." Pause. "Do you think I should write to him?" The words just came out of my mouth. I hadn't even thought them before that moment.

"Why the fuck would you do that?"

"I don't know. Just to . . . talk."

He sighed. "It's *your* job, man."

"I know."

"I don't think that would be cool. We're in training. They can fire us for, you know, looking funny. Saying the wrong thing." Smith was rail-thin and had sharp eyes behind his glasses. He was holding a cookie and gesturing with it like it was a power tool. "I don't think he would be all that interested in a critique from us."

"No, I would bet not."

"Funny, though . . ." He was thinking. Smith was the meanest, most sardonic person in the class, so I had naturally gravitated to him. Mean people keep you warm.

"What?"

"Maybe you could get the Mullet to do it." He smiled and bit through the cookie.

The Mullet was the resident weirdo of our training class. I found out later that every class had at least one. It's a side effect of a selection process that screens and selects for freaks: you occasionally end up with the wrong kind of freak, one who has antisocial tendencies in the extreme, or a funny smell, or that indefinable something that made villagers in the Middle Ages spontaneously drown certain folks in the local creek.

The Mullet had a mullet, naturally, but he was so much more than his choice of hairstyle. He practiced tai chi in the break room, an activity so repellently anti–break room that it set everyone's teeth on edge immediately. No one does tai chi at ten A.M. in front of their coworkers around a coffee kettle unless they want to be hated. He talked about fighting battles with padded staves in the Society for Creative Anachronism on the weekends and how they would drink homemade mead afterward and sing with someone's lute. His pants fit strangely around his crotch so that it looked like he had a constant, gigantic erection.

Geek Messiah

None of this was forgivable, but the real backbreaker was his behavior in class. After each point in the trainer's lectures, like clockwork, his arm would drift upward, he would sigh audibly, and then his voice would fill the room like the smell of rotted eggs: *"But I don't understand why ... blah blah blah ... if I had designed this tool . . . et cetera."* Like so many other geeks, the Mullet expressed his need for love and adulation by preening and claiming authority. He was king schmuck, and we all hated him for it.

It takes equal parts hate and love, I suspect, to really motivate employees. Just as Lee Marvin learned in *The Dirty Dozen*, having someone to hate unites the rest of the group. Some of us may have been resistant to programming and uncertain of our place in this bewildering crusade, but we knew with utter certainty that we loathed the Mullet. It welded us into shape.

Msmith's idea was that we would get the Mullet to write to Jeff, and the pungent force of the Mullet's personality would result in an instant dismissal. Like so many office vendettas this one went unfulfilled. No one wanted to talk to the Mullet for any length of time, even if it was for the good of the company and might help get him fired—it just wasn't worth it.

Jeff's email address was still rattling around my head once I was back at my seat in the training class. While the instructor gave another eloquent example of Amazon's inevitable victory, I fired up my email. It was near the end of training. I sat at my seat with the address I had typed in staring back at me

jeff@amazon.com

daring me, wanting me to say something, say anything, speak and press *send*.

I did not. I closed the program. But the next day I wrote a few lines and then put the message in my draft folder. Soon another followed it, and another, and I could not resist the pull of writing them, of writing to him. I didn't realize for a long time that I was falling in love.

▶ I vividly remember the first time I met Jeff. I like to believe we touched each other's hearts that fateful summer day, but I like to believe a lot of things and that doesn't necessarily make them so.

It was during my last week of training, which I took as an auspicious sign. At this point we were pretty certain that since we had not yet washed out we would soon receive offer letters and become full-time employees. The excitement of this development was tempered by the requirement that we work on express phones four hours a day out in the main room, an endless floor cut apart by cubicle walls as far as the eye could see.

Take the most boring thing you have ever done, double it, and you've captured the dynamic essence of express phones. In those olden days of the net there were a lot of people who did not trust computers to receive their credit card information when placing one of these newfangled Internet orders. This wasn't due so much to actual fraud occurring in great quantity as it was to the massive media coverage that the issue received, usually with headlines like: ARE YOU SAFE FROM THE CYBER-THIEVES? and WILL HACKERS STEAL ALL YOUR MONEY IF YOU TYPE THINGS AT A COMPUTER? Pop-culture tip: when the title of a human-interest story ends with a question mark, the answer is always: "Yes, and it could kill your children. More after the break."

As a result you could talk until you were blue in the face about rock-hard encryption, firewalls, isolated servers, and an impeccable security record, but people were still convinced that someone named SkoolK33dZ_57 would be buying Thai hookers with their hard-earned credit.

So those of us still in training, perhaps as a final breaking of our spirit, would have the following phone conversation:

"Thank you for calling Amazon.com, may I have your order number?"

"I don't remember that."

"That's okay!" (We were aggressively chirpy.) "How about your name?"

"Sure, my name is Some Bastard Ordering Yuppie Shit at Amazon."

"Okay, hold on . . . here you are. What card will you be using?"

"Visa."

"Okay, I'm ready for that number." This was the moment of truth—you wanted the words to glide out smoothly so they wouldn't put up a fight and ask you to prove it was safe.

"4426 6787 4513 7081."

"And the expiration date?"

"Oh-six oh-one."

"Great! Your order is processed! You will be receiving your Pile of Things in five to seven days via U.S. ground shipping! Thanks for calling Amazon.com! I will always love you!"

And that was it. To really get the feel of the process, remove all the humor from the above conversation, then get a friend and use it as a script—it should take you about forty-five seconds to get through. After a few tries you should be able to do it from memory.

Now keep having that conversation. Have it three hundred times. Take breaks between conversations if you need to, but time them to ensure that they don't add up to more than fifteen minutes. You'll find that your soul slips out of your body pretty quickly, goes for jaunts to escape the suffocating boredom. At least sweatshop workers actually make some physical object; express phone operators have nothing tangible to show for their efforts at the end of the day, not even a sneaker, and we had to live with the certain knowledge that what we were doing was error-ridden and pointless.

You see, each and every one of those callers could have entered his or her card number on the website, automatically encrypted and safely delivered, but they were all afraid. So instead they chose to place their orders over the net, call us at Amazon.com, and wait on the phone for up to an hour to give their credit card numbers to total strangers making waiters' wages without tips who would in turn write their precious bank numbers down on notebook paper.

Yes, notebook paper. A lot of hay was made in those days about how Amazon.com had turned database management into an art form, and Amazon was eager to perpetuate this illusion. After all, Amazon's technology was the most tangible of its ethereal assets—the one most often cited when stock analysts rhapsodized about the glorious future that lay in wait for the company. Brick-and-mortars had the resources and the market share, but Amazon.com had the technical brains.

The only stumbling block was reality. As would become clearer and clearer over the years, life at Amazon.com was one long, horrific emergency, an endless series of triage decisions made at breakneck speed. The fact that so many lucky guesses and gut instincts actually worked is testament not to careful forethought but to the battlefield efficiency and tenaciousness that Amazon sought in its recruits. Heroic IT personnel spent their days and nights handcuffed to systems that were constantly breaking down under ever-increasing loads. They were an army of industrious, bleary-eyed Dutch boys plugging holes in the dykes, praying for some never-realized downtime when they could finally make the systems work correctly.

Then, usually under peak load, the servers would seize, the build would break, one of a thousand balanced variables would go wrong, and the net effect would be the same each time: it was as if all those Dutch boys suddenly had their thumbs cut off, leaving them to stare helplessly as the waters rushed in. Not pretty. This happened constantly, and each time heads would roll. Amazon.com is the world's most aggressively marketed beta product, descending directly from Microsoft—where the original book on this way of doing business was written.

When the databases went down the effect was always the same for those of us in the trenches: we could do absolutely nothing. We couldn't answer a single question, fix a lost package problem, or even wipe our own bottoms. We were dead in the water. As a PR move we had a carefully rehearsed script: we would tell people who called that we were down for "scheduled maintenance" and that we would contact them shortly with the answer to their query. Occasionally someone would ask why we chose to do maintenance in the middle of the day—we'd laugh and say in one breath, "As-a-24-hour-global-provider-of-books-music-and-more-we-try-to-schedule-our-maintenance-periods-so-that-they'll-impact-our-customers-as-little-as-possible-I-am-saddened-and-disappointed-that-we-failed-in-this-case," and then promptly go to the next call and say it again.

If you were unlucky enough to be stuck on express phones during one of these outages you were instructed to say nothing to customers calling in—they were skittish about their credit cards as it was. Instead we took down their precious numbers on scratch paper so that later we could enter them into the database. Often the systems would be down for so long that you would need to take stickies and Post-its covered with tens of thousands of dollars' worth of transactions and put them in piles to be entered when and if anyone ever found the time. Sometimes people would forget and leave them at their desks—or even take them home. I used to find scraps of highly sensitive financial data in my pants, enough to go to Mexico and live extremely well.

The day Jeff walked into my life I had been on express phones for three hours and was solidly in the zone. It had been a good day—sharp calls, good pacing, and the Oracle database had not crashed, yet. My soul had taken a lovely walk down by the world-famous Pike Place Market and was ensconced at a particularly fabulous doughnut cart, where it languished, wishing my body could keep it company. That was how I missed the swirl of whispers, stares, and smiles that heralded Jeff's visitation.

I was sitting next to pperry, who in his civilian life went by Pete.

"Look!" he told me. I stared at him between calls, uncomprehending. All my higher functions were wrapped up in batter and waiting to be dumped into the sweet boiling oil of the fryer. I tried to speak.

"Thaaa. Thaaa. Whaargh?" *Lovely, lovely doughnuts. My pretties.*

"It's Jeff! He's right over there!" This was the most exciting thing that had happened during training—serious red-letter shit.

"Where?"

"Over by cdawson—by the door."

I have to admit, at first blush I was disappointed. I think I was expecting something more visible, like a nimbus of energy around his body or a halo of fire that would spell out BILLIONAIRE! over his head. I had been augmenting the propaganda we received every day with some websurfing and research of my own, so I felt as if I was already something of an expert on the subject of Jeff Bezos—a feeling shared by everyone in the room. It made it even more bizarre to see him in the flesh. You never suspect that Chairman Mao will be visiting *your* textile plant. How could you ever come face-to-face with your god?

This god came down the aisle between our tiny stations, seeming incredibly approachable. That was one of his most striking traits—he radiated easygoingness, which is remarkable for a guy who runs the most uptight company in the dot-com world.

He stopped by my station. He was going to speak to *me*. For a moment I was certain that I must have fucked up and sent him the email I had intended to keep secret . . . and even more briefly I found my heart lifting, hopeful that my exquisite prose and hipster flattery might have touched him deeply, just as he was touching me now with his soft brown eyes, that I had found a secret place within him that could see I was his son . . . his geekish apprentice, potential laying dormant, waiting for the firm hand of a true leader to whip me into a paragon of Amazonian deliciousness.

It all seemed possible in that moment as I experienced Jeff's gaze for the first time. Like great leaders and snake-oil salesmen Jeff possesses the uncanny knack of making those to whom he speaks believe that they are the only people in the entire universe—he can focus all his attention in the present and listen with such acute intensity that you are compelled to fall into him as he speaks with you. Steve Jobs at Apple has it, Clinton has it, Hitler had it, St. John the Baptist was swimming in it—call it the reality-distortion field. Saints and sinners all, the greatest and the worst . . . but Jeff is probably the most unassuming man who carries this gift within himself. He looks like the boyish uncle you adored as a child, who would never suspect just how seriously you'd take his every suggestion. He spoke, and his voice was clear, articulate, and completely unexpected.

"How is it going?"

"I'm in training." This did not actually answer the question.

"Great. Are you planning to stay with us at Amazon?"

I loved the way he turned the decision over to me, like a Scientology or self-empowerment guru who assumes that the world is simply about making up your own mind—there are no obstacles, only opportunities. Had I made my decision for Christ? For Amazon? I answered like an expectant bride: "For so long as you'll have me."

This made him laugh.

Jeff's laugh defies description. He is constantly laughing: it defines him. Many have tried and failed to capture that laugh in words, but all the similes and metaphors come up short. Let me try: Keep a child in a lightless box for a number of years and play the sounds of hyenas and Henny Youngman on a constant loop. Every couple of hours, whenever he seems relaxed, strike this child with a wooden stick. When you release this child at eighteen from the box, he will sue you for inhumane treatment and win. The noise the box child will make on the courthouse steps as he delights in the victory that sends his sadistic tormentor to the poorhouse for the rest of his life will sound a bit like Jeff's hooting, barking, and genuinely disturbingly arrhythmic guffaws.

Just as Jeff began laughing I could feel the atmosphere change in the room—something had happened. My first thought was that nearby workers were disturbed by the bizarre sounds coming out of our spiritual leader, but everyone was used to that. No, it was the system again—it crashed.

Jeff walked away toward other worker bees, still laughing, a kind word here and a thoughtful glance there as we scrambled to hide the wreckage as calls kept flooding through the dykes. Everyone worked a little faster than normal, a little more smoothly, to avoid showing Jeff that something had gone wrong; there was a slight smell of shame, as though we might have been the ones who knocked the system offline with a mis-placed phrase or a misdirected thought.

As the daily disaster unfolded I could not resist keeping an eye on him as he continued working the room, row by row through the cubicle maze, showing his honest and heartfelt love with laughter that simply would not stop.

➤ The day we graduated from training they gave us our offer letters at lunch, and we went to the afternoon session of class wondering what was left for them to show us. Trainer Mandy had left and instead we were faced with a pudgy young guy with bad acne and a nasal inflection—a genuine old-timer. All hail the early geek!

What followed was an unabashed lovefest for all things Amazonian as the old-timer took us on a walk down memory lane. We saw old versions of the website and giggled over a tool buried in the UNIX database that would compute your current stock option value. It was the most blatant round of propaganda yet—a few hours of war stories for the troops before they're sent into battle—but after four weeks of training we loved it. I loved it. I had visions of myself, years from now, coming to training classes and telling them stories of the old days, when Amazon didn't have branches in sixty countries and an exclusive contract to provide the U.S. government with reading material. I could taste it, and I had never been more ready to be a productive member of society. This job was going to be different. I would care. I could feel it.

After class ended we all went down to the Back Door Ultra Lounge and knocked back some drinks. The old-timer came and we crowded around him, fawning over him in our naïveté. Jean-Michele was downtown and joined us, sitting quietly, patiently, as everyone babbled about work.

On the way home Jean-Michele hazarded a few comments about what she'd seen. "People seem awfully positive."

"Yeah, it's nice." I had been drunk and effusive at the party and I could feel myself turning skittish. I was embarrassed by all the talk of invisible stock money, the geeking out, and the sycophantic toadying. Until a month earlier I had been an itinerant artist and unemployed layabout. I could feel my ideals rubbing against my motives like marbles grinding.

"You seem to be fitting in."

"What does that mean?" Instantly I was paranoid.

"It means that you fit in with this group. I've never seen you happy at a day job before."

"Well, it's a fantastic opportunity. A unique opportunity. A real opportunity. An opportunity." When I become unsure of my footing I often become forcefully repetitive.

"Yeah, looks like an opportunity." Jean-Michele sat watching me. That sounded critical. I searched for hooks in her voice, for doubt. Everything she said sounded like suspicion, an indictment of my choices. I wouldn't let go.

"How do you think I *fit in*?"

"You just seem to have a lot in common with these people."

"I like working for this company."

"Goodness! Things *have* changed."

"Things have."

She softened—she's very good at softening at dramatically appropriate moments. She lowered her tone, leaned forward, and said, "I'm really proud of you, Michael. It is a great opportunity for us." I hadn't realized how much I needed to hear her tell me that, and it wrecked me with a feeling I've rarely had—the sudden warm rush of earned and deserved praise. It felt so good to finally be doing something right.

Not everyone had such a great day. Pperry, who had alerted me to Jeff's presence, didn't graduate. They held him back for two weeks, something they did when the programming needed just a little more time to take hold. He was incredulous; he'd been a little slow on some tests, but he'd worked his ass off for weeks and knew the byzantine commands backward and forward. He didn't deserve probation.

I'd been seated next to pperry for the length of my training and could attest to his skill. He was, in fact, a lot better than I was, and I had cribbed off his sheets a number of times and probed him during breaks for details I'd missed while I was reading *The Onion* online during class. I started wondering how long it might take them to figure out that I didn't know what I was doing.

To: jeff@amazon.com
From: mdaisey@amazon.com
Subject: introductions

It's strange to be writing to you like this...it's so terribly intimate and sexy. Sure I've seen you walking among the cubes in Customer Service like some sort of saint, laying your hands on this worker or that, smiling and beaming--but I would hardly say that makes us close.

As you can tell from the header, my name is Mike Daisey and I'm a recent hire in Customer Service. If you were going to be dating me, I'd tell you that I'm 5'8", 250 lbs., have blond hair, deep brown eyes, and a hefty build.

I wonder who is reading this letter now: an email screening program, a personal assistant, or even, perhaps, you. I don't know if it will ever get through to you or if it will be stopped by a maze of permissions and denials set up over the distance between the places we both stand. Right now, as I begin writing, I wish I could tell you everything about myself, filter my desires into the ethernet of our local access network, rush it past the ten people who screen your email for crackpots like me until it lies supine and resplendent in your inbox. For all I know this letter will never be read, and that would probably be best for my continued employment.

It feels oddly natural to write to you. I don't normally speak much with coworkers, much less my boss, let alone a rock star boss who doesn't even know I exist. But I'd be willing to bet this happens to you a lot. I can imagine that the people in my training class and in the hallways are all writing to you, funneling you their secrets and their stories. I feel like it's encouraged, the way your name is invoked with hushed, familiar reverence--the way my grandmother used to talk about St. Peter. There's a kind of all-seeing, all-knowing aspect that feels true to me. My Own Private Jeff.

I read that story in WIRED where you were telling them that you wake up every morning scared, and that you hope every employee wakes up scared too, because we could just be a blip, an anomaly, a pebble in the waters, and vanish without a trace. I read that article twice.

You know, the real question is why am I writing you at all? I don't know, really. Truth is, I like you, Jeff, and I thought that I should make the effort to reach out. I imagine us trading emails, maybe getting to know each other: it could be fun. I could play the cabana boy and you could be the naughty CEO and it would be this sort of psychosexual romp, like a Cronenberg movie but with less bodily fluids and betrayal.

God, I sound so glib. The truth is that I worry about you. I hate the thought of you waking up scared every morning. You're under enormous stress, and everyone knows it, but you can't let anyone in, can you? One day your small balding head is going to pop off your tiny overcaffeinated body and that will be the end of everything. Well, I won't have that-- not on my watch. Please let me know if there is something I can do from here. Please know that this employee thinks you have built something special, and everyone I work with knows it, and I think the world is going to know it, too.

md

5

Our Physics

There is more than ideology involved in running a company, even a dot-com. Every company is a social animal, and the pressures of the marketplace create laws that define how jobs will be done, where the shots will be called, and who will get the really comfy chair in conference room B. We all lived by a kind of dot-com physics. To delineate its laws would require a more supple and cohesive mind than mine—but this aesthetics major will give it a shot.

Time Dilation

This is the principle that, owing to this damn relativity of the universe, as you move closer and closer to the speed of light, time gets more and more vertiginous. People call this distortion "Internet Time."

You remember Internet Time—it was very hip in 1999 for about four months. It was the height of hot—every business magazine threw the term on its cover like oregano, hoping to spike its sales. Boardroom captains basked in the idea that the New Economy was so radioactive that time itself would twist to serve its need for speed. Why do one thing if you can do two? Three? Four? How fast is the speed of thought? Let's find the limit.

The high holy grail of time dilation was multitasking—the method that would allow you to have your leisure time and your work time in equal proportion because you would play *while* you worked. Middle managers were expected to carry on email conversations with subordinates on their web-enabled Palm (strategy) while watching the opera (culture) from box seats where they'd cop a quick feel of the girlfriend with whom they used to spend quality time (biology).

It was the old American Dream rewired for the twenty-first century: it was no longer hard work and perseverance that would win the race, but efficiency. Efficiency became so sought after because it seemed to provide a justification for the psychotically escalating race: if we were simply efficient enough, we'd be able to outrun the edge of failure, even when the debt was mounting and the future was unknown. If you kept hustling hard enough, you would find the cash somewhere. If you couldn't, you must be a lazy or inefficient bastard, because it wasn't conceivable that the task was impossible . . . why, that would mean that the whole enterprise, this whole machine, might be rushing too quickly forward with no one watching the bottom line, or that there was no bottom line, nothing firm beneath the juggernaut, and that was simply unthinkable. You'd never get up in the morning.

So all the cool kids tried to be on Internet Time and live their lives enslaved to their peripherals 24/7. It caused no end of problems for many firms: everyone would be asking, "Where's Larry? Where is he? Goddamn it, that presentation to the investors is in an hour!" And poor soon-to-be-ex-vice-president Larry would be a blur, moving too fast for people in his own office to see, jumping and waving, shouting, "I'm right here! Look at me! I've been to lunch four times today! Jesus! I've got twelve more meetings in the next seventeen minutes, so I'll take them two at a time, one on each ear! Internet Time! I need to vaccinate my chinchilla! Ah! Appointments! Christ!" Bad scene—folks couldn't synchronize.

Amazon workers never suffered from this because everyone was on the same platform—Amazon Time. And everyone believed in Amazon Time not as woolly abstraction but as unshakable fact. We were all moving at this sickening, accelerated, and unreasonable rate together, aging at the same incredible speed like that bad *Star Trek* episode where the comet makes everyone old.

This showed up most strikingly in the obsession with counting dog years. Conventional wisdom held that Amazon Time was equivalent to Dog Time, which meant that one human year equaled seven Amazonian ones. You lived through a year and you might look twenty-four, but you were really thirty-one. Do two and you were as good as thirty-eight, even if you still got carded buying booze.

Actually, it was more complicated than that. Early in my time at Amazon somebody emailed around an article from the

ASPCA that detailed, year by year, exactly how Dog Time translates to Human Time. As it turns out, puppies age very quickly, but the process slows down as they grow. It quickly became a time-killing fad: everyone was constantly calculating his or her exact dog years, down to the minute, mailing around automated scripts to do it on terminals, chatting about it in the lunch room. It became a badge of honor, to have done so much time, another in-joke in an already insular community. If we all hadn't been so chickenshit whitebread, we'd have been tattoo-ing tears on our faces—one for every calendar year—the way they do in prison.

The prison analogy works precisely because it is so melodra-matically overblown. We were all techie yuppies in training, not criminals, and we were doing time in this company because we believed in it and believed we'd be repaid in riches—but there was always an aura of desperation and enslavement in the air that was missing from other dot-coms. We took joy from our drudgery, even as we sighed and rolled our eyes over all we had to do. There was a deep masochism involved—after being a slacker in the workplace I was perversely delighted to be living for the office, and everyone around me was slaving too, always harder than I was, it seemed. Everyone got into it, spending ever-increasing amounts of time talking about how damn hard we were working.

Did we really work that hard? Once I would have sworn to it, but in hindsight I can't see the timecard for the hype. Maga-zines, television, and the web told us every day that we worked harder than anyone else, and we drank that in as sweet affir-mation of our certain success. Our pride came from our belief that we were the hardest-working company in the world.

We loved to grouse and complain. "God, it feels like I'm aging." "Me too." "Me too." "Are you miserable?" "Yes, I haven't even seen my children." "I don't even have time to have children." "God, I'm miserable, but I'm with you." "Yes. We have each other." "I love you." "And I love you." You get very close to the people around you because you understand one another's suffering so intimately, understand the motives that make people work nights, work Saturdays, work when no one needs to work, work for pleasure. You're in cubes instead of a foxhole, but hey.

Jean-Michele's grandfather, Babcia's husband, was called Dziadek, which of course means grandfather in Polish. When he first came to America he worked for years and years in a steel mill, making a quarter an hour, eating salt tablets to survive the heat from the blast furnaces. Dziadek passed away before I met him, but I think he'd have been proud of me for working at Amazon—and I suspect I'd have been quieter about my long, grueling, air-conditioned days.

Xeno's Paradox

The second law was Xeno's Paradox. It's an old mathematical conundrum that I first heard about in the seventh grade. I mention this because it is the only thing I learned that year and I am thrilled that it has shown such unexpected relevance.

A runner is in a marathon. Every hour he covers one half of whatever distance remains. So first he goes half way, then there's a quarter of the way left, then an eighth, then a sixteenth, then a thirty-second, a sixty-forth, a one-twenty-eighth, a two-hundred-fifty-sixth, a five-hundred-twelfth . . . he gets closer, ever closer, but though the goal line is an increasingly infinitesimal distance from where he stands, he can never quite seem to get there. He'll keep rubbing up against the boundary like a cat, shave the distance down to within a half of a hairsbreadth but won't ever reach it.

That runner is your strike price.

A quick definition is in order. Your strike price is the price the stock was at on the first day of your employment. Since your dot-com is presumably going to appreciate in value like a cure for cancer, the lower the strike price, the better. If you have a low enough strike you'll be worth millions before you've finished working six months.

I don't know how many times a week each of us would say, "Jumping Christ! If only I had stopped looking at porn and playing Sega and just started working at Amazon *three months earlier* . . . I would be so rich now! What was I thinking?" But this did not take into account the effects of the first law: due to time dilation those three months could be the equivalent of more than a year and a half—a full generation in the tech world.

This led to bizarre conversations in which grizzled twenty-seven-year-olds told dewy-eyed twenty-five-year-olds over bottles of rotgut whiskey, "Well, you got here in *August,* but I've been here since *April,* and let me tell ya, things were *different* in those days. Harder, more rugged, not like you pussies have it now. Back then I used to do all my coding by hand, without computers, on these clay tablets here. Then I'd load them onto my burro, Pepe, and take them down to the steam locomotive so they could travel across the continent to the compiling factory. Now *that* was how you ran a business!"

Ridiculous? Certainly. Seniority was a fact of life at Amazon, and we accepted it. Due to the cataclysmic rate of growth and the riches that accrued to people with low employee numbers, we all worshiped "old-timers." Being closer to the beginning was like being closer to the sun—people regaled each other with stories of knocking back beers with Jeff, or hanging out with the first coders and those who would be movers and shakers. You got extra credit if you didn't have to ask who those other characters were, and few did. We all knew our Amazon mythology backward and forward.

It would be nice to believe that this was simply due to our love for the company, but a lot of it was awe of success. In the dot-com world the normal rules of status were boiled down to nothing more than your hire date—who you were and what you did mattered a lot less than when you did it. An old-timer who lifted boxes in the warehouse was worth millions more than a newbie executive. The early heroes were all worth astronomical amounts of money—in some cases hundreds of millions of dollars, staggering market capitalizations that choked up calculators.

So a patina of fame clung to the old-timers—they lionized their contributions, exaggerated their exploits, and made every employee who came later feel, frankly, small-dicked. You couldn't help but compare yourself to these mammoth organs that lorded over the landscape and know that no matter how hard you might work you would never be worth a fraction of what they already had.

It was a temporal caste system, and despite repeated claims that we had an egalitarian workplace it infected every relationship. If you knew when someone joined the company, then you knew what their strike price was, and if you knew what their strike price was, then you knew what they were worth—and we know from our capitalist society that if you know what someone is worth, then you have them by the balls.

The Heisenberg Happiness Principle

I'm actually just making up this physical law and basing it on the Uncertainty Principle by the same author, which posits that we can never actually know exactly where any particular particle in the universe is located because the act of observing it makes it be *somewhere else*. You can know one or two of the variables, but you'll never be able to pin the sucker down—there's an unshakable aura of uncertainty and doubt that surrounds every electron.

The Heisenberg Happiness Principle is important enough in understanding Amazon's situation that I will pull it out from the text and let it stand on its own:

As the uncertainty about what Amazon.com is rises, so rises Amazon's stock price.

Jeff has always been very forthcoming about what Amazon is *not:* parrying doubtful analysts' statements with heartfelt and convincing explanations of why Amazon is not a bookstore, a physical store, a media company, a preference aggregator, a retailer, or anything else that can actually be assigned a value. By clinging to its own definitions of what it was, and then not sharing those definitions with anyone else, Amazon became the only arbiter of its own success or failure. Politicians know this instinctively—control the battleground and you have won the war before it is even waged.

Here's an example: in the early days everyone was certain that the company would be crushed when Barnes & Noble entered the web, that their brick-and-mortar dominance would pull customers from Amazon. There were numerous articles: AMAZON.GONE, AMAZON.BOMB, and other terribly clever headlines in that vein. We know what happened: Amazon was not crushed at all, but rather beat bn.com by virtue of having been on the web first and having much better customer service and a more user friendly website, all in all creating a much better experience.

But "beat" in what context? B&N still has all its physical stores, and even if the website isn't growing at a staggering rate it's not as if B&N's physical store sales have been crippled by Amazon. People still like going to bookstores, which strangely is considered more romantic than spending an evening alone in your underwear staring at a website.

As soon as it became common knowledge that Amazon had whipped bn.com's behind, the next logical step was that Amazon would have to take on the mothership—Barnes & Noble itself. If Amazon was going to justify a market cap larger than most third world countries, it was going to have to trounce Barnes & Noble and all the other physical booksellers, since books, after all, were Amazon's core product.

But just when these sentiments might have started appearing in the press, Jeff swerved. B&N was never really a competitor, he let it be known. Reporters would ask about the rivalry, the dueling press releases and other PR efforts of the past, and Jeff would shrug and smile his smile. He talked about entering new markets, how Amazon was so much more than a bookseller that it seemed book sales hardly mattered. It was as though he could hold up a hand puppet and tell the press, "Look at the puppet . . . don't look over there, look at this shiny puppet," and the press watched the puppet, wondering how on earth he made that little guy talk. You wouldn't even know that Amazon sold books anymore from some of the stories coming out, much less that they were the vast majority of its sales.

Jeff knew Amazon would never be able to compete with Barnes & Noble, and even if it tried, it would have to do so by buckling down, focusing, and sacrificing momentum in new areas. That would lead to clear projections, comprehensive assessments of the future, concrete ideas about how much money this machine might produce—all of which would undermine the horrifically huge stock price that was needed to fuel the growth that fueled the stock that fueled the growth that fueled the stock . . . and so forth forever. Better to sidestep the question and leave everyone perplexed and guessing than cop to solid numbers—that would kill the dream, and the dream was what kept everyone happy, workers and investors both.

By avoiding every attempt to define the company Jeff brilliantly wrote his own dance card. Losing $1.38 for every dollar coming in became an acceptable profit margin when you were talking about a vast, unknowable revolution that required sacrifice to obtain market share. So long as the stock kept rising, the human pyramid of institutions and investors would trust one another with fear and bravado, eyes closed and hands on their guns, hoping never to see a sign of weakness. So long as nothing slowed there would never be a reason to collectively pull the trigger. No one wanted that, and there was strength in the human desire to avoid unpleasantness at any price until the last possible instant.

Of course, given the nature of physics, the inverse of the Heisenberg Happiness Principle was also true. Every time Amazon released a number or disclosed a fact, it became vulnerable to a kind of economic inertia and was pulled toward earth, its stock slipping in fits and starts back toward reasonable human expectations. You can't run a publicly traded company in the dark, at least not forever, and Amazon.com was aging according to its own accelerated clock. The more people knew, the less they'd want to play an expensive game with hot-air stock. Time was not on Amazon's side—Jeff would certainly agree with that.

Silence Is Golden, Like Handcuffs

Silence ruled the day at Amazon. The PR department inculcated us with the belief that the press should never be trusted and that the outside world—with its emphasis on "profitability" and "balance sheets"—was evil and never to be listened to. This allowed Amazon to be consistently *on message,* synchronized with the latest developments on how great, fun, super, and cool Amazon was. Not only did the silence help the company work in the outside world, it also made certain that Amazonians ignored anything negative they might hear coming from beyond the walls, keeping them internally and eternally *on message* as well.

Consider how the soaring stock price was handled. It was obvious that the stock was a huge element in the company's success and that it was an effective recruiting tool—it got people thrilled about working there. Despite this, discussion of the stock was not tolerated either in official channels or off the clock. Everybody might be getting rich, but there was to be no whooping, hollering, or talking about it. Shh. Don't be happy.

This was so at odds with reality that it created a schizophrenic aura around everything stock-related at Amazon. We were all glued to the ticker, day and night, but we also followed the party line, which meant we copied Jeff. And when Jeff was asked about the stock, he would feign ignorance, ask where it happened to be, and appear utterly nonchalant to the fate of billions of dollars in equity. So publicly we tried to pretend not to care as well.

Jeff proclaimed that you shouldn't judge your performance by your share price. If you got twice as smart when the stock doubled, you'd also have to become half as smart when the stock nosedived. This was a sober and responsible way of looking at things, but Amazon had built its infrastructure, incentive programs, and entire engine of success around the ever-growing stock price, which made the hypocrisy of expecting the employees to ignore the numbers ridiculous. How could the employees ignore the one number that topped every story on the company, stories that arrived by company email to their desks each morning?

It was also hard to ignore the fact that supervisors and those only a little more senior than you would suddenly buy houses, boats, and ski lodges. While Amazon wasn't exactly minting millionaires in CS, people there were still watching their net worth balloon—and a lot of new horizons open up when you make nine dollars an hour, but on paper you could have $400,000 cash in just four years.

It also caused incredible waste and confusion, since the company had no culture of support for those who cashed in their stock. There were old-timers at the warehouse who took the great wads of cash and held parties every night for six months, only to discover that there was this thing called "taxes." Everyone knew that Amazon stock would keep rising for the life of the company, so they didn't do their math based on what was in their grasp, but instead on what all their options would be worth in five years.

It had certainly changed my life. I had no more cash than before, but the constant promise of future money was reassuring, like a vacation you are always just about to take. It was better than real. A sense of financial security was the steel behind the velvet warmth of the Amazon family.

They call these "golden handcuffs," although in CS they were more like silver ones: few had access to immediate cash, but a better life for all seemed to be just around the corner, not to mention the promise of possibly rising into a position in corporate. There were undocumented tools in the server system installed by anonymous benefactors that let people calculate options and strike price data. Everyone had the stock bookmarked and tickered, secretly fed to them moment by moment.

This covert behavior intensified ten- or a hundredfold if you were actually selling some of your stock, because selling the stock was considered a minor form of treason. People who admitted selling would feel obliged to explain in detail why they had sold, how they hadn't sold much, how they still had faith that better times were ahead, and soon. You could sell some, but you always hastened to express how you had much, much more that you would never sell. People blame greed for the reason many ended up with nothing, and that certainly played a role at the top of the heap, but it's not the whole story. Pride, guilt, and belief had a large part to do with why workers didn't sell out the stock they had and walk away with more winnings from the dot-com lottery.

The Missing Fifth Force

Physicists are always searching for the "fifth force"—a force that many of them believe will tie up a lot of the loose ends to our baffling universe and explain inexplicable behaviors. The fifth force that ruled Amazon.com is such an ancient chestnut that I hesitate to bring it to your attention: You can fool some of the people all of the time, and all of the people some of the time, but you can't fool all of the people all of the time.

Another name for this is common sense, and by August 1998 everyone who had it in the tech industry had been roundly condemned as Chicken Littles or reactionaries and shot. The few who escaped were run out of town on a rail after getting tarred and feathered for being loathsome "value investors," old fogeys who didn't understand how the world worked now. Pundits who espoused these views were laughed at in *Forbes* and *Business Week* for not understanding the new physics, and despite the public humiliations, they took their winnings quietly off the table in the belief that they had been lucky to escape.

That wasn't us, of course—why would anyone ever leave? You'd have to be a coward, no, a *traitor* for not believing in the future. Even when it was torture there was a sleight of mind at work, as when a magician shows you the cloth, the table, the beautiful girl, and the rope he uses, but never all of them at once. Never that.

6

College Years

To understand what customer service at Amazon was like you need first to understand the landscape it inhabited, both physically and spiritually. First, banish all standard notions of dot-com architecture—no high-rises, no sexy racquetball courts or meeting rooms with Jacuzzis. This was Amazon, and that meant strict furniture puritanism. A company that builds all of its desks out of doors has a high ethic of cheapness to uphold. The same was not true in every part of the company, but they'd never let the phone monkeys see that.

Central to the nature of CS was Amazon's incredible growth rate. As we were very fond of telling anyone who would listen, Amazon was "the fastest growing company in the history of the world," which certainly sounded true, even if I had no idea what metric was being used to support the statement. When I joined Amazon there were around three hundred employees, and when I departed there were over six thousand. For a time the number of my coworkers would double every six weeks. Amazon was dedicated to growing its employee base as quickly as its stock price.

The facilities department, responsible for housing these folks, was constantly being reamed with impossible problems to which Amazon expected a can-do solution yesterday. The downtown vacancy rate in Seattle was astronomically low, and as the dot-com explosion spread, spaces became even more scarce. It had not dawned on anyone at Amazon that they might need to plan for the numbers of warm bodies being brought on board—due to the continual state of emergency, no one had time for that kind of meddlesome accounting. Because of this, facilities had no idea how much space it was going to need.

So facilities scrambled, eked, and blind-ass guessed most of the time, and quickly entered into long-term, binding real-estate contracts. Sometime early on they picked up the Securities Building, a dank fortress of sixties architecture in downtown Seattle. It became the staging ground for Amazon's swelling CS department.

Amazingly, Amazon had managed to find an office building that had no windows. It was a rat warren of a building where I spent my days and nights in near-total darkness. There's some precedent for this—CS call centers I have visited at other companies also have no windows, though I can't see how depriving your employees of any sign of the outside world makes them motivated or efficient. It might have been the classic box trick—remove all outside stimuli and you have a better chance of inspiring monomania.

Worse, every last cubicle was decorated with piles of kitsch: *Star Wars* figures, secret decoder rings, retro lunchbox collections, piles of marbles, bad fantasy art. Christmas lights climbed over everything, absolutely everything, and it was required by old-timers that they remain up all year long. The place was a nightmare omelet of the trashiest contents from every dorm room across America. When they've taken everything from you, all you have left is your dignity, and we happily traded that away for a Limited Edition Boba Fett Action Figure.

There were some remarkable feats of adaptive decorating. Two different people had padded flannel "dens" under their desks, so that they could take naps. A few other desks were covered by elaborate pagodas—they became miniature caves, lit from within by blacklights or monitor glow. One person grew grass all over his desk with the use of peat moss and grow lamps; it was a tiny garden in the big black room.

OK, it wasn't completely lightless—on one wall there were four small frosted windows that served four hundred of us. They weren't terribly clear or clean windows, but never in my life have I witnessed such machinations for sunlight. Grown men and women cried, schemed, and had knife fights with letter openers in the bathrooms, where unscrupulous managers would take bets on who would be killed and who would walk away triumphant with a seat that received a few feeble rays for a few hours a day.

Exacerbating the absence of sun was the fact that no one turned on the lights. If you dared to flip the switch—maybe it was your first day and you didn't realize that you would be expected to work in the dark—someone would rise shrieking up out of the cube warrens: "OFF! OFF! TURN THE HORRIBLE LIGHT OFF!" And you did that right away or who knew what would happen? Eventually, old-timers unscrewed the bulbs to keep the fresh meat from assaulting us. We just didn't like light anymore. Every day, leaving the building, it was the same: "God! No! It burns me . . . !" And this was in *Seattle* sunlight—had the call center been in L.A., I assume we would have burst into flames.

This phenomenon had a lot to do with the thriving Seattle goth population, all of whom had found a home in Amazon.com's CS department. It made sense that Seattle and Amazon attracted goths—the city hardly has any natural sunlight as it is, and goths don't object to "selling out" the way that hardcore punk followers do. They like to work days so they can stay out all night, drinking wine in cemeteries, powdering their faces, and generally being gothic.

If you ran through the hit parade of other Amazon customer service social groups—computer geeks, movie-trivia freaks, English Ph.D. candidates—you quickly discovered that sunlight was not a big priority. These were people who were long on high-speed Internet access and short on love of the great outdoors. Since the fluorescents were regarded as "ugly, soul-killing light" that only office workers would tolerate, we elected to work in darkness—or by the pale phosphorescence of monitor glow.

A big perk of working CS was that no one ever saw you, which allowed a lot of alternatively dressed people suddenly to have a shot at upward mobility. It was strangely dislocating to look around and see a multiearringed goth mama sitting next to the boy with green faux-prison facial tattoos and the dyke with the cheek piercing who had shaved her hair into the shape of Captain Picard's face, speaking clearly and confidently to Mrs. Williams of Sheboygan, Wisconsin, about the lateness of her order, thanking her effusively, begging her to try Amazon again in the future. If you've called, you've spoken to them, though you'd never be able to tell the difference between them and a vanilla CS rep like myself.

I had never seriously considered the question "Where would I be employed if I had the words HELL KITTEN tattooed across my forehead?" Getting said tattoo would certainly be a career-limiting maneuver. That's why Amazon seemed so miraculous. Here you had chosen to cast yourself out of American society, and here was this company that would still give you a 401 (k), decent pay, and, glory of glories, stock options . . . all because no one would ever see your face.

But as with all unspayed cats, the number of Hell Kittens grew exponentially. Eventually, finding places for folks just to stand was a challenge, and CS was inspired to come up with "hot desking"—derived from the "hot bunking" practiced on submarines. Owing to limited space, sailors share beds on staggered shifts: as someone is slipping out of a bunk on his way to man the radar, another is coming to bed after running the engine room. CS management loved the expression because it sounded like war talk, which they already aggressively employed in their pitches to CS employees. We were "troops," the upcoming Christmas season was "the war," and now we would not have the one dignity afforded other office drones, our own desks—but it was OK because it was called "hot desking" in the memos. Cool jargon and the right spin will get groups to accept just about anything.

I never met my deskmate, which I found peculiar—her shift started right after mine. I knew her login was ginal, so her name was probably Gina L., and she had bubbly handwriting and a picture of Commander Riker from *Star Trek* within a heart-shaped frame hanging in our collective cubelet. The picture had a small candle in front of it, creating what I feared was an ad hoc shrine.

I didn't really want to meet her—I loathed the Riker that

stared at me twelve hours a day, and as soon as I could I brought in mounds of office supplies from my home stash and artfully arranged them throughout the tiny space, covering every surface to ensure that no further shrines could be erected.

Jean-Michele didn't understand why I needed three different styles of stapler and a minishredder in a paperless office, and when I explained she was contemptuous.

"You don't have your own desk? Where do you work, a sweatshop?"

"No, there just aren't resources now. Space is tight, and we all have to make sacrifices." I was cribbing bromides from World War II newspapers.

"Oh. That makes sense," she said, though she meant the opposite. "I just thought you'd have money for things like *desks* and *windows* since the company is worth more than Sears. How can you be valued so highly as employees *and* be left without a place to sit? Why don't they just spend some of that huge cash war chest you told me they have?"

"It's complicated."

She understood too well. I remember thinking, *I'm saying too much, explaining our finances too much. I need to give out less information.* With Jean-Michele I thought this. God help me, it builds itself up in the bloodstream, one molecule at a time.

—▶ Actually it *was* a bit of a sweatshop, or like something from the accounting halls of Dickens's *Bleak House*—a wasteland of cubicle dividers filled with the ceaseless murmuring of order numbers and apologies. If human misery and efficient boredom could be beautiful, there would have been a kind of beauty in the endlessly replicated, hot-desking, rack-mounted workers and their swiftly exchangeable work stations. Lit up by the dead light of our monitors we would constantly scratch at our keyboards—it could have been sadly romantic, if it hadn't been for the sirens.

Hanging everywhere were readerboards showing the number of calls on hold and the average response time. When the numbers got too high they would turn red and a fearful, piercing whistle would go off, hooting over and over. People developed neurotic aversions to the sound, they shook and looked up like dogs when they heard it.

Msmith explained it to me. "It's conditioning."

"What is?"

"The sirens. They actually condition you to work faster."

"Uh-huh."

"No, I'm serious. Think about it: what's the most horrible sound you can think of right now?" The siren was blaring right over our head—*eepEEP, eepEEP.*

"I think that would be the siren."

"Right. They make it horrible so that you feel intense relief when the siren stops. . . . Wait for it . . ." The siren stopped. "See? Can you feel that?"

"Holy shit." Sitting there, I could actually feel my heart rate dropping and my tension beginning to dissolve. "It's like I'm wired to it."

"Yeah. I heard they could have gotten a normal alarm, but the workflow analysts they hired said we'd work harder if we had something at stake."

"Damn." I didn't know what else to say.

Msmith smiled. "You going to the quad potluck?"

"Oh, I thought I might."

This was a joke. Potlucks were social activities in customer service, and in customer service social activities were far from optional.

Our lives were structured around the "quad," a term of unknown origin that signified a manageable clump the size of a squad or platoon. CS management broke us up into these groups to manage workflow and to make certain that everyone had someone with an eye on them, but mostly it just helped create job positions above email gerbil to which people could aspire.

Each quad had a "quad leader," and the quad leader had two lieutenants known as "leads" who were there to provide guidance and be leaders-in-training with ill-defined job descriptions. In addition, quads had six Tier 1s (greenhorns) and six Tier 2s (veterans). It was very much like a combat team, sans guns, combat, and machismo.

The weirdest thing about the entire structure was how totally unnecessary it was. We never spoke to anyone on our team with regard to our work. You were surrounded by coworkers but you never needed to have meetings or "interface" with anybody. The only people you spoke with were four to six hundred customers a shift, on the phone and via email. Every couple of days you might have a question, but you just asked whoever was next to you and they'd tell you what to do.

Dividing us into small groups did make it easy to keep us occupied and happy, a godsend to CS management. Our supervisors were required to organize extracurricular drinking nights, social activities, potluck lunches, and special outings. We named our quads after pop-culture detritus: Graceland, Route 66, Area 51, *Barbarella*—the list was endless. I lived in Dagobah, Yoda's swamp.

I still remember every quad meeting I ever went to, since these were the only times we ever spoke on the clock. We always started by introducing ourselves: name, title, last book read, favorite movie moment, and favorite ice cream flavor. People always said them in one run-on sentence:

"I'm Jacob Hadster Tier 1 Joyce's *Ulysses* when Luke says 'Nooooo!' in *Jedi* and Mocha Almond Fudge Chip."

"I'm Noelle Berry Tier 2 *Wuthering Heights* the last ten minutes of *Cinema Paradiso* and New York Super Fudge Chunk."

"I'm Mike Daisey Tier 1 *Microserfs* the opening scenes of Kurosawa's *Yojimbo* and plain vanilla."

This getting-to-know-you game was judged necessary because of massive growth—quad leaders wanted everyone to know everybody and have a great time. New people came in so often that you generally only knew half the people in your quad, and in the three weeks since the last meeting the other half had been promoted up and out to other positions as leads and supervisors.

In many ways quad leaders were more cruise directors than supervisors, albeit cruise directors on a dank and windowless boat. Very little actual business was ever transacted—there'd be an advisory about something, some goofing around, free cookies. So much for the combat squad.

The games were all familiar—they could have been lifted from the microivy I went to, or from other college freshmen orientation exercises at overpriced whitebread colleges across the country. It made sense: you had overeducated people who didn't fit into the corporate world living next to each other, and they were all in their midtwenties. All of them. College was the only social model that made sense, and it was there in force.

So we bootlegged Sigue Sigue Sputnik albums, showed each other rare *Ranma ½* episodes, and those who weren't previously attached spent every waking moment sleeping with one another. Since the normal social order had broken down, the only people we had anything in common with were other Amazonians. There really wasn't time to find love or a life outside the company, and in the New Economy we were learning that enlightened folks slept where they worked—why shouldn't they take all their other pleasures there too? At least our fellow workers would understand the dead-fish skin, bleary eyes, and confusion about sunlight.

I knew I was not in Kansas anymore one night at a house party for three different quads, watching a supervisor chug beers while my teammates cheered. Others who were busy making out with coworkers may not have realized it, but I had logged enough time in corporate America to know that this was very, very wrong. You weren't supposed to be doing tequila shots at make-out parties with your supervisor. Amazon CS was half socialist book camp and half college party dorm, a combination which should have delighted me to no end.

Instead I was heartbroken. The more in love with the company I fell, the more it was clear that I was terrible at my job.

➤ At first I had a thousand excuses—I was tired, it was a hard week, I was still getting into the swing of things. I made these excuses to myself, then to Jean-Michele, then to my coworkers. It was when I had to begin making them to my quad leader that I knew things weren't going to work.

I was a terrible customer service representative. I didn't have the attention span, the detail-oriented nature—I was a flake. I would promise people that they would receive their book in two to three days when I knew it would never arrive—I couldn't bring myself to make them feel bad. I gave book recommendations off the cuff rather than following standard protocol. In fact, I started telling people when I didn't like their book choices. I gave refunds to people I liked on a whim and sent them their books anyway. I gave refunds to everyone with a Polish last name, or if I liked the gift message they enclosed. I sent unrequested copies of the The Illustrated Kama Sutra to priests. I was getting sloppy the way unprofessional drunks do when they're looking for an intervention. I was cruising for termination.

I tried talking about it to Jean-Michele, but that was painful—I'd been so publicly enraptured with living up to my obligations that I was afraid to reveal the depths of my incompetence. It was also hard to explain that although I loved and lived for Amazon and talked about it incessantly, I couldn't actually hold a job there. It was as if I was angling to become a booster for Amazon rather than an actual employee. I didn't realize it at the time, but what I was hungering to become was a dot-com executive—the best job a dilettante could ever aspire to, and one for which I was uniquely suited.

I was never going to get that opportunity, I knew that, and I wasn't even going to survive at the company if I didn't find an angle or edge. As much as I believed in the cause and pledged myself daily, my contrary nature kept asserting itself.

The problem was that I hated the customers. As I spoke with Mr. Mathers of Winnipeg, whose Complete Works of O. Henry was unaccounted for, I wished I could trace his number and hunt him down in his ski lodge. I daydreamed that I'd beat him to death with O. Henry, shouting, "Here's your 'Gift of the Magi!' In your face! Booyah!" I reasoned that if the customers would just shut up and go away, we wouldn't have so many system problems and my job would be a lot easier. Since we lost money with every shipment, hell, why not stop altogether and get off this ride?

I think folks in customer service jobs all over America eventually hit this wall. Faced with the ceaseless flood of email and the phone calls that literally have no event horizon, they realize that this will never end, ever, and nothing they do will ever make it better. Someone will always be screaming for help. Social workers have a similar problem, although their sense of connectedness is stronger: saving a crack-addicted mother beats "We've located your Power Ranger set!" any day of the week.

In the end you either rise above it with some degree of grace or are crushed beneath. I began practicing magical thinking even more than I normally do—I tapped the table three times between each phone call, I made a hash mark on scrap paper for every email, then walked around the room after every hundred, I started leaving porn on my screen hoping someone would catch me. Nothing kept my rage and boredom from growing. I had to get out, and as in Dante's *Inferno* the only way out was to go all the way to the bottom and find an exit. I had to be promoted into corporate, out of this sweatshop and up to Amazon's beautiful headquarters overlooking the city.

The trouble was that Amazon hated promoting people out of customer service. Not only did they have would-be employees constantly scrabbling at the gates, but CS was filled with low-class freaks and geeks, and the khaki-clad über-techies weren't very hot on sharing their lofty heights with this kind of rabble. A lot of the useless hierarchy within CS was designed to keep us from rioting.

To help ensure that they got what they needed from you, Amazon customer service required a one-year minimum "indentured service," which, I swear to God, is the language they used when I asked about transferring to a different position in any other department. Oddly, that hadn't been addressed at the orientation meeting with the great-smelling, clean-skinned people who had waxed ecstatic about boundless opportunity.

I was caught—there was no way I could serve out my tour of duty. One year/12 months/52 weeks/365 days/8760 hours/

525,600 minutes/31,536,000 seconds. At my pace that would have been 204,400 emails, which worked out to approximately 10,220,000 words—which would make 170 books the size of the one you are reading now. According to the ASPCA/Amazon Time scale, the first year is equivalent to fourteen years. In dilated time I would be thirty-nine, and looking at a midlife crisis. Every day as I woke up I knew I wasn't going to make it. Everyone else knew it too.

To: jeff@amazon.com
From: mdaisey@amazon.com
Subject: transformers, dreams

I'm really not meaning to intrude but I have to ask: what's wrong with your money? You drive an old hatchback and rent an apartment. I know you are trying to "keep it real," but it seems grotesquely modest given the enormous power and influence you should be wielding.

The truth is (and you shouldn't be ashamed of this) you're worth between $6 and $40 billion, depending on how many people like you on any given day. We can't even comprehend that number--you could give everyone in America enough money for a hotel room, or conversely, you could get a $130 hotel room for yourself every night for three million years, longer than the human race has been around.

I guess I don't understand why you don't *do* something with all that money. You're a geek from way back--it's why I'm so drawn to you. I love your childhood, like the school for gifted students you started, and the crazy inventions you used to build, like that solar-powered windmill. You're like Tom Swift mixed with Richie Rich and a dash of Napoleon.

That's why if I were you I'd take $10 billion and

dump it into building an enormous robot body. Maybe it was watching THE TRANSFORMERS at an impressionable age, but I think a gigantic metal robot with tremendous strength and stamina would be a killer addition to your wardrobe, and you could change your name to BEZOS PRIME or DECEPTIBEZOS.

You think I'm joking, but this is a real opportunity: eventually your puny human body will wither, but as BEZOS PRIME you could have your brain uploaded and walk the landscape fighting BILL GATEICUS for control of the Pacific Northwest. That would rock.

You're our leader, like Jesus or Ronald Reagan-- where's the awe and kick-ass splendor? Or at the very least, get your Palm Pilot built into your arm and make it run off your body's magnetic field, like that atomic watch you already own. Damn, that thing is cool, the way it synchronizes with the atomic clock in Denver 36 times a second. If I were you, I'd have one on each arm and both legs, and then check my pulse a couple of times an hour.

It's funny, I have this recurring dream. I'm in a BizDev meeting room with you, and you're all the way at one end of this enormous table. I run up toward you while you're explaining how buying superassmonkey.com is a great idea, and I whip out a wicked knife from nowhere and cut off your hand. Your left hand. I grab the hand and run out of the room, across the cafeteria, past the guards who are

Subject:transformers, dreams

shouting, and out the doors as the PA keeps sounding, "DANGER. JEFF'S HAND HAS LEFT THE BUILDING. DANGER." You're all behind me, spilling out of the building like so many ants, but I'm running too fast for anyone to ever catch me. I'm out on the lawn, eating your hand, hungry like I've never been in my life. I eat the whole thing, chew through the bones, and now I own part of you, just like you own the best part of me. I wake up so indescribably proud.

md

7

Gorillas vs. Bears

My doppelgänger in customer service was Warren. I'd known him since college—we'd both gone to the same microivy, and while I had managed to graduate after a scandalous fifth year, Warren had burned out and flipped off the institution after two. He joined Amazon a week after I did, having snowed the temp company on the subject of his bachelor's degree. Warren was like me in that respect, but once he got to Amazon he functioned on a whole different level.

Warren was a cowboy. Warren was badass. Warren was the way I *wished* I could be in customer service—endlessly competent, chain-smoking, and hard drinking. He was the Johnny Cash of customer service, if you can imagine such a thing. Warren was the best customer service rep ever to work at Amazon.com—loyal, inventive, rule breaking, and sharp as a bowie knife.

Warren's secret was that he had a sublime and deeply mystical connection to the essential nature of customer service, which is, at the dawn of the twenty-first century, America's unofficial religion. It's a perverse communion. The Cuisinart breaks, the stain-resistant carpet fails to resist a stain, your precious book from Amazon.com is late: if you are like most consumers, you would rather die than face the horror of a physical world that does not conform to your whims, especially since you've paid Good American Dollars for it to do so.

Luckily, you do not need to take responsibility for your possessions—this is America, and we are blessed with Customer Service. This means the Customer is King, and that means that someone, somewhere, is responsible for this unspeakable failure. It's not only your right, it is your *duty* as a consumer to find the mandatory 800 number and ask the company in question What They Intend to Do to Make Things Right.

At the same time, consumers who call to do their consuming duty by complaining don't really expect anything to be done, and they are right—nothing will be done. You will not get a new Cuisinart, carpet stains will not disappear, and your books will not come any faster than they were going to before you called.

What you will get is the opportunity to put your foot on the neck of someone else who has a job just like yours—because everyone in America is doing customer service for someone else at this point, either in name or spirit. You can't actually get anything fixed, but how cathartic and necessary to be able to be the oppressor for a day, to put your foot down and apply that firm pressure, to feel someone's voice on the line apologizing, trying to make everything right for you—a promise they can't possibly fulfill.

Warren was the chain-smoking Yoda of customer service. He understood all things, understood that the sounds at the other end of the line were not people—they were simply disembodied voices that let loose an endless stream of abuse, hatred, and shit. He understood that his job was to drink in this shit, pour it through himself—take it into his body, take whatever they were giving out. He didn't process it, he just funneled it down, squeezing it low, coiling it into his lower kundalini, curdling it with his libido, compressing it into his gonads, filling his balls with impotent hate, and containing it there. Holding it all down below allowed the rest of him to sound clear, resonant, and apologetic. Very apologetic.

" . . . I'm sorry to hear that. I'll tell you what we're going to do, we're going to remove the shipping charges for that and I'm very—

" . . . All right, I understand, I understand that that won't help, I understand. I empathize, I understand, I'll tell you what I'm going to do, I am going to go across the street to Borders right now, I'm going to purchase that book with money from my own wallet, I'm going to express ship—

" . . . OK, I understand, tell you what—I understand. I empathize. I understand. I empathize. I'm sorry. I'm going to tell you what we're going to do, I'm going to go home now, I'm going to sacrifice my firstborn son on an altar of my own making. I just hope that my son's death will in some small way show you that we know how unforgivable it is for us to be late with your Harry Potter book."

He was simply breathtaking, and as a result he rose and rose through the ranks until he occupied an exalted position in customer service, outside the usual quad bullshit. If you called Amazon.com and you were a true asshole, not a jerk but an Asshole, this great thing happened to you called "escalation." It really should be called "hot potato." Escalating means that the first person can't deal with you because of your freakiness so they throw you to someone higher on the totem pole. Code for this on the phone is "Let me transfer you to *my manager.*"

While there was a set protocol, it usually wasn't followed—many times we just found someone near us and said, "Hey, want to be my manager?" If the other guy was in the mood for a laugh he'd agree, and suddenly he became Mr. Big Shot High-Level Bureaucrat in the Executive Resolution Department who could finally render some assistance. Never, ever believe that you've reached an actual manager when you complain to anyone in customer service—customer service's job is to take the bullet so those managers won't have to speak with you.

Now if the caller is really angry they're going to go up, up, up the ladder, and if they're still a really big Asshole, they'll get escalated many, many times so that everybody sitting around in CS can take a turn. In addition, if the caller is entertaining enough, employees make up bogus departments just so their coworkers can talk to people like Benicio Del Toro or the German who talks like Snuffy Smith.

I don't even know how many levels this goes on for—maybe seven or eight or nine—but back then, the end of the road was Warren. Warren was the Alpha and the Omega.

You see, Warren loved difficult calls. Loved them. Confronted with his rich rolling baritone, unshakable logic, and rock-hard documentation, even the most blazing psychotic would mellow. He parlayed this unusual skill into a unique position, a combination of troubleshooter and customer assassin. If you called Amazon and bitched enough, he was where you'd end up, and his wrath was swift and just.

He dealt with all the great ones, like Tommy/Tammy, a man who would torture customer service workers for pleasure. He'd make up orders, pretend to be other people, change identities during calls, scream, and froth at the mouth. His real name was Tommy, but he'd try to convince people that he was Tammy. Warren wasn't having any of this.

"Hello? This is Tammy. . . . I don't have my order number, I lost it—"

"Tommy, we know that it's you. We told you never to call here again. We don't want your business."

"I'm not Tommy, I'm Tammy—"

"Shut up, Tommy. Listen." Warren was unfailingly polite and resolute. "You're not to call here anymore. We don't want your business, we're blocking your number, don't ever call us again. Don't ever order from us. Please order from our competitors. Goodbye, Tommy." Click. And that was the ultimate reason to be Warren: if you rose high enough, you could take all that hatred you'd been stewing in your gonads and finally shoot it at the people the company told you it was OK to execute.

He also dealt with the Cackler, who would call innocent customer service reps all day long, one after another. They would answer the phone—"Thank you for calling Amazon.com, can I have your order number?"—and then they'd hear this unearthly, high-pitched psychosexual panting, as though the caller were an extra from *The Silence of the Lambs*.

"Have . . . you . . . ever . . . seen . . . *The* . . . *Wizard* . . . *of* . . . *Oz*?"

(A moment of silence ensued while the CS rep consulted his mental three-ring binder of approved and certified responses.)

"We, uh, we have it on VHS and DVD."

"I . . . want . . . you . . . to . . . cackle . . . like . . . the . . . Wicked . . . Witch . . ."

Warren got tired of this pretty damn quick. Thanks to his troubleshooting position he had the ability to trace where calls came from, so he did a little research and then gave the guy a call to say hello. He got the Cackler's parents. In his best Dirty Harry he told them, "Your son is calling our people and trying to make them cackle at him. I'm afraid we can't allow that." Silence. "There are numbers that your son can call and be cackled at . . . but none of them are toll free."

All Hands Meetings were the glue that held Amazon together. These high-energy love-ins resembled no other company's annual meetings—and Amazon upped the ante by holding them four times a year.

Owing to our astronomical growth, each quarter the meeting was held in a steadily larger rented space. It was a three-hour affair, so everybody got coffee and bagels at the door, dot-com soul food to survive the onslaught of fun and charts that would follow.

Don't get me wrong—I loved the All Hands Meetings. They were fascinating, they made me feel great about working at Amazon, and they got me out of half a day's work. It was this reality-distorting heroin that would help us true believers last out the next three months. We were an army in khaki and Dockers mixed with tattoos and blue hair, squinting in the too-well-lit room, nodding smugly at the latest PowerPoint presentation laying out the details of our multinational reach, growing and stretching taut like a pregnant lady's belly.

When I went to All Hands Meetings I sat with Warren. He'd moved to the overnight shift, which meant he got off work at eight A.M. and had time to down three or four gin and tonics with his crew before rolling over to the convention center. He was trying to keep a low profile after the last All Hands Meeting, at which he'd arrived in an even more altered state of consciousness, leading him to shout, "HELL YEAH!" in his room-filling baritone after every bullet point.

Jeff had been unsettled, comments were made, and CSers were gently rebuked—so Warren was sticking with just one class of pharmaceuticals that morning. He was not happy about it. I thought he had it pretty good—all I'd had was a fucking bagel and coffee.

"Daisey. Are you ready for the festivities?"

"I suppose." It wouldn't be cool to admit you loved All Hands Meetings too much. "How you been?"

He looked like he wanted to smoke. "I feel like the French in '38—prissy and waiting to be creamed. We're not ready for Christmas."

"Yeah, I know. Everyone is running scared. Did you follow that Blodgett business?"

He nodded. "That guy's going to bury us with good intentions."

Henry Blodgett, may his name be forever accursed and his testicles eaten by pigs, was perhaps the most darling of the New Economy talking heads. When he made a pronouncement about a company its stock would soar or dive like a pet bird on a string. He had said a lot of great things about Amazon and had set a ridiculous twelve-month stock target. The overheated, ADD-afflicted market drove the price up to his projected level within a few weeks, absurdly fast. It was beyond absurd—it was criminal. He made some noises about it being "rather quick" but didn't lower his projections. We were really happy about the stock's high price—ecstatic at what it might mean in the long term. But this had jacked up expectations for the Christmas season past impossible to ludicrous.

"We're going to have to sell Rolexes and Palm Pilots to every site visitor to hit these revenue estimates," I said. I wanted a Palm Pilot. Maybe I should buy one to support the company? I had no schedule to keep, but they looked so sexy—I could enter "WORKING" in all the days, Monday through Monday, so I would know where I was. I could web-surf on it when I left my terminal for coffee breaks. I really wanted one.

Warren looked at me. "Yeah, but if we do . . ."

"If we do what?"

"If we hit those numbers—we get the product out the door, we can win."

"And if we can't . . ."

"Then it'll be over." He rubbed two fingers against his thumb. "The creditors swoop in, the momentum gets shattered, stock falls, options fold, and the whole fucking thing comes down in pieces."

"Isn't there a middle ground?"

Warren laughed. "Shit, Daisey—what company do you think you're working for? Middle ground? Next you'll expect a pension."

"Forgot myself."

The hall was almost full now. In a few minutes it would begin, following a soothingly familiar pattern. I was worried that Warren would start shouting when Jeff came out—sometimes these things had weird, big openings, which focused the energy of the audience into a big yuppie geek laser, like a U2 concert for accountants, and that could set him off. Strike that—given U2's position in pop-culture as the flabby, decadent grandfather of style, it was *exactly* like a U2 concert. Spectacle, flash, and faux glam—it was all there. Except that this show involved big houses on islands and mountains of imaginary cash instead of leather pants and prepubescent girls.

"Warren?"

"Yeah."

"What's with Jeff's gorilla and bear thing?"

Jeff was the centerpiece of these events, crowd-rousing, laughing, making us do the wave, and letting us all in to bask in his coolness. He'd answer questions put to him in a fireside chat segment that featured a fantastic fake fireplace. For obscure, unknowable reasons he had a favorite question that someone would ask at every All Hands Meeting—the question and the answer were always the same.

Question: *In a fight between a lowland silverbacked gorilla and a Canadian grizzly bear, who would win?*

Answer: *Depends on the terrain.*

We would all laugh very hard and look knowingly at each other, but I have no idea what we were supposed to have known.

"That's a good question, Daisey. I have no fucking idea."

"It feels like it means something—am I crazy about that?"

"No. It has"—he gestured vaguely—"an aura of significance."

"Like a secret message."

"Or a plan."

"Maybe it's an allegory. Maybe he's talking about the tactics of being on the web in retailing. Maybe it's like everyone is asking, Who will win, Wal-Mart or Amazon? And maybe he's saying that the answer has nothing to do with the question—that it's a trick. It's not about comparing paw strength and jaw size but location and positioning. Or maybe it means that all that matters is what arena we're dealing with—the landscape defines the battle, like a Sun Tzu kind of a thing only with bears and gorillas. So if one of these bears has a slingshot, for example, then that is one tough bear because he has these ranged attacks, so you think he's going to bite you but instead he chucks a rock at your head, and you're a gorilla and you're like 'Shit!' because it's outside your paradigm. This crazy fucking bear is fucking with you from a distance, and you're like 'Damn!' because you know that this is how people are going to take care of business, you know, on the web, because we need to be the armed bears. Bears with guns, the bears who came equipped, or we'll end up being the gorillas who get their asses kicked."

I had proven once more I shouldn't think before a second coffee. Then the lights went down and the show began.

➤ I still don't know what the gorilla vs. bear anecdote means. I don't even know if it means anything at all. I do know that we all raised our eyebrows and nodded sagely when people referenced it. We did the same for buzzwords and phrases that others said over and over until we said them perfectly. When an industry is built on expectation alone the lack of tangible reference points creates an insider language that's all nuance.

It might just have been the latest rage in a long tradition of capitalist guru worship: line up to listen to the latest wise billionaire. Whatever George Soros or Warren Buffett said after dinner became gospel because they had *made it,* and the rest of us watched them from a distance, respectful, hungry for any inspiration that they might throw off like radiation. Or maybe Jeff was laughing because he had no idea what the damn story meant either, delighted at the human desire to find meaning in meaninglessness. Maybe that's the lesson. Take your pick.

1-Click™ Christmas

Everyone at Amazon hated Christmas. Years later, I still hate Christmas. It's collateral damage from having weathered the yearly storm of rapacious shoppers, apocalyptic pundits, and suicidal initiatives proposed by brain-damaged marketing flacks. For six or eight weeks you never actually went home. It was just like summer camp, but it was held every winter and the only activities were answering phone calls from angry people or packing books for angry people. Fourteen hours a day. And between warming up before and cleaning up after Christmas, the holiday lasted seven months.

I should be thankful for Christmas—I know for certain that if Amazon hadn't been in full fight-or-flight survival mode for the holidays when I started seriously fucking up, I would have been fired. My manager said as much. With Amazonian panache, I was told:

"Your performance is still suboptimal, Michael." He sighed, looked at me with his left eye, then his right eye, swiveling his head back and forth. "It simply isn't adequate." Translation: *You worthless pig-bastard, you waste of skin. How dare you sully our land of righteous customer service? You do not love Jeff as well as we do, you slacker, you dilettante. You suck.*

I had been dreading this evaluation for weeks. I was in trouble for good reason, and I was trying to be contrite without confessing to any of my more serious policy breaches—like sending free books to people I found in the customer database from Norway, which filled some dadaist need in me.

This had a rather quixotic origin. I had led an ardent crusade in college to convince friends and strangers that Norway didn't exist. You see, I believed that what we call "Norway" was a massive fraud perpetrated by unknown people for nefarious and underhanded purposes. I suspected the Dutch, because no one ever suspects the Dutch—the Dutch are a thin-lipped and parsimonious people. I had not forgotten their exploits in the sixteenth-century Caribbean. "Beware, for the Dutch never sleep" is a motto to which I ascribe.

Although there was a lot of anecdotal evidence that my hypothesis was valid—lutefisk, fjörds, the Norwegian "language"—I did outgrow this juvenile obsession. And by way of oblique apology I thought some of the good people of Oslo could use philosophical books that would affirm their own existence, as the dark Norwegian soul often finds itself plunged into existential conflict. In print, I again apologize for doubting you, Norway. Viva Norway!

I figured had I been outed on the free books to Norway, we would be having a franker exchange, but this hadn't come up yet, nor had my habit of photocopying my hand many hundreds of times—another potentially deal-breaking behavior. Apparently they needed each and every able body, even mine.

As the droning went on, I felt as angst-ridden as any conflicted Norwegian. I loved my company, but I hated my job. I wanted to be part of Amazon, but I wanted to avoid carpal tunnel syndrome and phone neck. I'd been seduced—not by the lure of getting rich quick, but by the idea of doing important-sounding things quickly, with a lot of electronic gadgets and a leather-grain briefcase. I wanted to be having fun.

My manager looked me up and down and said, "We'd like to give you a second chance," and I was glad, so glad, because beneath the bravado and silliness, I desperately needed to make this job work. *I'd like to be able to make a living doing something. There must be something I can actually do.* I promised sincerely to try harder, and I would: Christmas is no time for paying your respects to Norway.

➤ Just after Thanksgiving the call would go out to all nonessential personnel (read: anyone with a salary who wasn't customer service or warehouse) that they would be shipped out to work in distant Amazon distribution centers through Christmas. Corporate wage slavers would kiss their lives goodbye and head off for scenic outer Delaware and world-famous Town Twenty Miles from Reno.

Amazon had built their warehouses where the economy was depressed and labor was cheap. It hadn't foreseen how difficult it would be to find seasonal temps in these same areas, which made it impossible to staff the megawarehouses, some of the largest in the world, with enough workers—so Amazon's midlevel managers had to fly out and pick up the slack in an epic version of "everyone lend a hand and we'll raise this barn in no time!"

To say there was culture clash would be to put it mildly. Managers earning six figures were subordinate to warehouse leads whose last policy decision had been taking the doors off bathrooms to keep workers from shooting up on the clock. The web of loyalty and the work ethic that was indestructible in Seattle was shredded here, where no one received enough stock to give a damn. There were exceptions—when Jeff visited the warehouse in Kansas he got standing ovations and the workers begged him to sign their hardhats—and Amazon made certain the cameras and reporters were there to watch it unfold.

It's a simple equation: when a job must be done and there aren't enough people, the job still gets done. Failure isn't an option when failure equals death—this was a war after all. Amazon opened the floodgates at Christmas and everyone leapt to the fore. Many desk jockeys came apart performing manual labor in warehouses for sixteen hours a day, because doughy white office folk aren't capable of continuous heavy lifting over those kinds of periods. We'd been nurtured since college to sit immobile, moving only sixteen knuckles and the occasional thumb. When put to the test our knees explode in truly spectacular ways.

I didn't get to go to the warehouses; I was essential personnel, trying to hold down the phone lines as angry hordes of dissatisfied customers endured multihour hold times. It was an often debated topic at Amazon as to which was worse: the warehouse or customer service.

On one hand there was Delaware, exploded knees, and hotel rooms. On the other there were tens of thousands of people telling me how I was responsible for the unaccountable absence of their Waterproof Dancing Space Dog. After the parents had finished dishing out their rage they'd put their children on the line. These kids would talk about how much they wanted that Waterproof Dancing Space Dog and what the Space Dog would have meant, if it had come, if it hadn't been lost by you, the man who ruined Christmas. Between their sobs and whimpering I began to hate all Space Dogs, waterproof or soluble, and more important to hate children, especially those who cried. It hardly mattered which job was worse—no matter what flavor of poison you chose, you were still poisoned.

To say there was a shortage of manpower would be a gross understatement. As Christmas neared I found myself begging friends and family to come on board for emergency training so that they could help hold the barricades. I am told by others that they were repelled by my eerie intensity and the suggestion that somehow they "owed" it to Amazon to help. Jean-Michele got it the worst.

"Okay, so what exactly are express phones?"

"It's easy and fun. People call in, they want to give you their credit card number. You take it down and send them their stuff. Easy."

"I don't know. It's bad enough that I'm never seeing you. I don't really want to work on the phone all day in that weird dungeon."

"But it's fun! Think of Norway!"

"That Norway thing is stupid."

"Forget Norway. You could make nine dollars an hour."

"You just want company in your consensual hallucination."

But when I told Jean-Michele that I might not be able to make it to Christmas Eve, she was far less amused.

"I do not understand," she began, "how it is possible you could be telling me you might be missing *Christmas* in order to take phone calls from people who are complaining that their Christmas was ruined by your stupid company? Explain that."

"Well, I—"

"I'd like to know who I should call about *my* Christmas being ruined—is there a special number for us, or should I just wait on the main line?"

"I'm not working on Christmas Day—"

"We're Polish; we celebrate on Christmas Eve. *You* will be at that celebration."

"I'll try to, but—"

"No. No. Listen to me." Standing in our kitchen, I could actually feel her channeling Babcia. "This is bullshit. Quit."

"What?"

"Leave. You made more money temping anyway. This isn't worth it."

"What about health insurance?"

"You never go to the dentist anyway." That was true—I had been too busy.

"The stock—"

"Look, I'm just saying that you had better be at Christmas Eve. I don't care how you do it. Use some of that Amazonian ingenuity or bribe somebody, but just do it. If I hear you utter one more word about sacrifices that need to be made for this fucking Kmart, I swear to God I will walk out of this apartment so fast you will have whiplash."

Christmas Eve with Jean-Michele's family was wonderful that year.

➤ Instead of calling the insane overtime mandatory, which it was, management called these extra hours "suggestions," which was OK since we were all clued in and knew what pill we were swallowing. It would have seemed disloyal to ask Amazon to hire more people to make certain they didn't actually work someone to death. We weren't profitable, after all, so even thinking such thoughts smacked of laziness. We had doors for desks and we would make do.

There were always a few jokers who didn't get with the program. One day in the middle of the Christmas rush I got the lowdown from msmith, who was looking as pale and rubbed-down as I was.

"You're kidding? The Mullet?" I was flabbergasted.

"Yeah. They made him a lead."

"Damn. He can't even talk to people without offending them!"

"I know."

"He smells funny and he touches himself when talking to women!"

"I know."

"He has a mullet, for Christ's sake!"

"I know. And all that may be true, but the fact remains that he has become a lead, on his way to quad leader, long before either of us."

"Well, I *am* a total fuckup," I conceded.

"I heard."

"Great." I had hoped something could have remained private here. "What about you? You're behind too." In the hyperaccelerated world of Amazon, after three months we both should have been climbing the rusty career ladder of CS.

"Eh." Msmith shrugged. "I'm not a superhero—this place blows. I just want my cushy transfer into anywhere else."

"You and the rest of us. So what's the rest of the story with the Mullet?"

"This is where it gets good." Msmith leaned forward as he got into the story. "He gets the promotion, right? Like two days later he tells his quad leader that he is going to go home for the holidays!"

"No!"

"Yes!"

"Was he joking?"

"No. The son of a bitch gets promoted and then he's all 'off I go to have a holiday and see my family.' Like that's possible or something. Total crap."

"So he's denied?"

"Oh yeah. Instantly and with prejudice for even asking, you know?"

"I bet. I bet he started doing tai chi there in the supe's cube, to vent his negative energy the way a true Jedi would."

"Heh." Msmith actually laughs that way, with one syllable. "So he gets pissed, and guess what? Now he's refusing to do overtime!"

"Are you shitting me?"

"No, he's only doing forty hours."

"That is amazing. They can't fire him?"

"No, apparently not—it's Christmas, and that might look bad. But everyone around him is giving him the evil eye, and a couple of guys have been snatching his stuff, hawking loogies in his water bottle. People are pissed. Stuff like that. It's pretty weird."

We sat there silent for a while. The yuppie food dispenser, from which I ate a Chicken Orzo Salad with Almond Slivers and Poppy Seed Dressing like clockwork every six hours, ratcheted up and began to hum loudly. Someone else must have taken something from it and would be eating at their desk even now. Maybe a Tuscan Lasagna with Feta and Olives or the Mozzarella, Basil, and Arugula Herbed Focaccia Panini with Gingered Aioli. I thought of all the Chicken Orzo Salads I had eaten in the last ten weeks. I wondered if the makers of the

Chicken Orzo Salad knew that somewhere there was someone for whom their product was the center of his life. I had the sudden desire to write and tell them this, instantly followed by the certain knowledge I was wasting my life.

"You want to hear something fucked up?" msmith grinned.

"Sure."

"Last week my quad had a movie night—we watched movies in the quad, you know, at our desks and during breaks?"

"Yeah?"

"*Brazil.*"

"Whoa."

"We saw *Brazil.* I cannot tell you how weird that was."

"I bet."

"You know what was weird? No one else thought it was weird."

"That's impossible."

"No, I mean they knew it was weird, and everyone was commenting on it, like 'Oh, *Brazil,* hah hah hah, how droll.' But no one thought it was disturbing, honestly disturbing, to be answering phones and working here, in this place, and watching that at the same time. No one—I don't know. I can't explain it. Do you . . ." he hesitated, for the first time. "Do you get what I'm saying?"

"Yeah. I do. You know I do."

"Yeah. This fucking place."

"Oh yeah."

I didn't have the words then—I was in the middle of Christmas hell, and Amazon was my entire life, swallowing up all the pieces of me, and I wanted that, hungry for a new identity I could fall in love with. Msmith was talking about the sideways glance, the self-knowing chuckle. It's the most primitive type of irony, crass laughing to show everyone else you "get" what is going on—you "get" that Amazon.com is like *Brazil*, and since you "get" it you're immune. To name it is to own it—ollie ollie oxen free, you're safe. Since you're very, very smart and well read you can laugh at the misfortunes of others and your own situation. You're far too clever to be caught doing anything stupid.

Now I know differently. Just because you're in on the joke doesn't mean you aren't being laughed at.

To: jeff@amazon.com
From: mdaisey@amazon.com
Subject: oompa-loompa

No one else knows how you do it. When you stood on
those pallets of books fifteen feet high in Kansas,
the warehouse workers roared like you were Elvis
himself, all swagger and slickness and whiplash
smile. We pounded our hands together at the last
All Hands Meeting as if our clapping would add our
own small names to your Hall of Fame.

But I know how you do it. You make us believe we're
on that stage with you.

It's the essence of your charisma. Your joy and dis-
covery are so genuinely infectious that we're suddenly inside your life, looking out at our upturned
faces and risking everything on a magical scheme.
It's that smile, the boyish grin and "aw, shucks"
enthusiasm that you dole out--some for TIME, some
for CNN, some for the workers and the investors and
every last blessed customer.

But, it's getting hard to live on that alone. You tell
us again and again that the newest people we hire are
the sharpest and most qualified ever, and I believe
you--I'm not even a year in and I feel ancient and
slow compared to these greenhorns who had to beat out
hundreds to get a stab even at data entry.

The older you are the more you feel it: the pressure that you won't keep up with Amazon's competency curve, that it will pass beyond your own event horizon and leave you stranded, not qualified to pump gas for these hyperaccomplished Ivy League ADD cases. No one could compete--these people were MBA candidates in utero. They eat their babies for breakfast.

It's hyperdarwinism--you can actually watch as the ideal Amazonian worker evolves from moment to moment, losing its gills, walking on land, and learning to code before lunchtime. I suspect you've designed it this way, because if we burn through personnel the way we burn through cash it'll be that much easier to bootstrap Amazon up from garage-operation-done-good to multinational Wal-Mart.

Things keep changing, which I know is supposed to be "dynamically exciting," but I can't tell where we're going from one day to the next. When I joined, this was "Earth's Biggest Bookstore," then we were "Books, Music and More," and now we're "Earth's Largest Selection." Largest selection...how vague is that? We're getting so big so fast we have to use slogans that specify nothing. Next we'll be "Large, Large Thing."

Also, the new customer service management team has been telling us we're a "preference aggregator" rather than a retailer. I think it's one thing to sell this bullshit to the press, but we're trading in the college party people for pseudomystical doctrine spouters.

I realize I'm betraying my old age with some of these complaints, but you need to know. You're our Willy Wonka, Jeff, and we're your Oompa-Loompas--the orange midgets who dance, torture bad children and make candy. You saved us from the Vermicious Knids and gave us a place to live and work too. You granted us all Golden Tickets. We trust you, because you told us to trust you, and we believe in you.

I always loved Wonka, both the books and the movie. My favorite part of the movie is when Wonka puts everyone on the boat and they sail into the dark tunnel. Suddenly, for this one scene, it isn't a children's candy film anymore as strobes flash and images spray over the boat, visions of worms crawling and women screaming.

It's Gene Wilder who makes it unforgettable. He starts quiet, with his eyes open and luminous, but his voice soon rises and rises as he speaks in one unbroken breath about how he can't control the boat, how he doesn't know where they are going. He's screaming at the children as the boat plunges into the darkness, everyone lashed to the ride. I think Wilder should have gotten a fucking Oscar for that.

md

Subject: oompa-loompa

9

Mission Statements

I had been in customer service for six months and I knew that I had to get out. After Christmas there would be a lot of confusion, work pileups, and the inevitable backlog of returned items to deal with, but once all of that had been taken care of the eyes of management would find me, standing naked, ready to be taken out to the woodshed and horse-whipped. Though I had been perfunctorily diligent during the monomania of Christmas, I had not gotten consistently better, and with the pressure off I was slipping already, headed back to my old ways like a drunk to the bottle. It's a sad state of affairs to be addicted to incompetence, but such is the fate of those who are honestly bad at their jobs.

I'd like to think that if things had been different, I would have done well in customer service. After all, I was in love with the company and you would think this would have pushed me over some vital edge and into the realm of "passable." I'd like to believe that, but it's simply not true. And the reason that I'm scientifically certain it's not true is because of five numbers that Amazon measures:

1. the amount of time you spend on each customer call
2. the number of phone contacts you have in an hour
3. the amount of time you spend on each customer email
4. the number of email contacts you have in an hour
5. the aggregate sum of the number of phone and email contacts you make every hour

Those five numbers are who you are. They are, in fact, all you are. The five numbers are just the beginning of metrics, and it is the Devil's work.

Metrics will do exactly what it claims to do: it will track everything your employees do, say, and breathe, and consequently create a measurable increase in their productivity, sometimes by as much as 10 percent . . . at the small cost of all their human dignity. As customer service matured at Amazon they used better and better metrics, sharpening and closing in on an exact quantification of each and every worker's productivity.

The sad thing is that metrics works so well precisely *because* it strips away dignity—it's that absence that makes it possible to see precisely who is pulling his weight and who is not. Yet I believe that the social contract of the workplace is predicated on certain mutually assured delusions, and one of the most necessary delusions is that *we all believe we are competent at our jobs.*

We need that illusion, desperately and completely. Everyone does—even you, dear reader, do not want to be incompetent. We all know the incompetent people—they slouch through our lives everyday, disrupting the flow of our perfect wastepaper basket shots, screwing up everybody's good time, making a nuisance of themselves. They are the 10 percent of people who cause 90 percent of the problems, and on bad days we all look at each other, grinning and shaking our heads over how these pitiable specimens ever came to be entrenched in a pleasant hierarchical bureaucracy like ours.

No one wants to be known for being bad at their career—at a job that they have been doing for eight or nine years, for forty or fifty hours a week. It's hard to have an excuse for that kind of ineptitude. It can be a horrific epiphany to empirically discover your exact place in the office universe. Ultimately, that is what metrics does: it makes the implicit office pecking order explicit. People discover exactly how much work they do, how well they do it, when they do it, and how often they take pee breaks while it is being done. Saying it's Big Brotherish doesn't go quite far enough—it's more like having to sleep with Big Brother nightly, and then, after he's finished having his way with you, watching as he whips out a cigar, lights up, and tells you in Technicolor detail just what your faults are in bed.

It made me Jekyll and Hyde pretty severely. On weekends I loved Amazon and I would speak at great and windy length to many people, especially relatives—"God, I love my company, I love working, it's so great, we're making history, we kick ass, it's so great, I'm great, let me tell you about this new product category"—until I realized I was starting to bore even myself. It was addictive though. People would ask what I did for a living and I actually had something to tell them. More than that, they actually looked interested, wanted to know what the company was like and the story about that stock. It was like dating the sister of a very famous person—the flow of residual fame was invigorating.

But when I came into work I flipped—while there I hated the place, hated the phone and the email and the endless tracking. Most of all I hated meeting with my supervisor, because at Amazon there was never a positive reason to have that meeting—it is always punitive when metrics exist to show where to bring the hammer down.

My second supervisor, Samantha, was an oddity. She had warm brown eyes and looked the part of a hippie earth mother but was extremely dedicated to playing her role as a corporate metrics enforcer. It was kind of like having Jerry Garcia come after you for tax evasion, and then after the shock and the laughter is over, discovering to your dismay that he is very good at nailing you for IRS violations.

There were more than a few neo-hippies at Amazon—they came for the same reasons the goths and other subcultures did: acceptance and stock options. They dreadlocked their way through the days, ate dolphin-safe tuna, and talked about nuclear disarmament while listening to their new Rusted Root CD. It did lead to some bizarre and irreconcilable collisions in philosophy, however: Samantha was Michael Moore's biggest fan. She loved all his work, read everything he wrote, believed everything he said. The fact that Samantha then spent her time tracking every moment of her subordinates' workdays, issuing warnings for "excessive bathroom breaks" and practicing secret surveillance checks apparently didn't generate any kind of cognitive dissonance for her—she was blissfully irony free.

It's too bad she couldn't appreciate how perfect the joke would be—a year later the world's friendliest New Economy company was waging an anti-union campaign cribbed from General Motors, complete with mandatory "information" meetings and constant alerts from management about how unions could only endanger job security. They certainly could: a month after the union failed, Amazon chose to terminate all of Seattle's customer service workers. Some were let go immediately, including several vocal union sympathizers; the rest were kept on for a few months to train replacements in North Dakota and West Virginia. The majority of their jobs were sent to an email center in India, where Amazon had discovered they only needed to pay a dollar an hour for that most American commodity, customer service.

I often wonder how she reacted to this, knowing now that the management she supported eventually used the terribly accurate metric data she gathered to find a group that could give service ten times cheaper. I like to think that her barrier to irony is intact and that she still doesn't realize what she was doing—she's a really nice person at heart.

I was glad that she had taken over as my supervisor because I felt that I was having more luck pretending to be a model citizen under her watch. Still, there were problems. The following is a verbatim transcript of one of our meetings:

"We've been tracking your work since the last meeting, and, ah, you are number 163. Uh . . . that's you right here on this chart. See? You're not the worst! There are actually about eighteen people below you, you see that there? Uh, but that's you, right there. So, as your supervisor, uh, I'm gonna keep having these meetings with you, and we're gonna talk about what to do about this problem. Um . . . I think we, and by 'we' I mean 'you,' should try answering *more* emails and taking *more* phone calls . . . um . . . and maybe you could do them *faster.* That would probably make this number go up, and that's, I think, what we're looking for, for this number to be up . . . as opposed to . . . um . . . down. Make sure it doesn't go down—that'd be my advice. That wouldn't be good. Well, we're going to be meeting weekly at this time from now on to discuss this. I'm really glad we had this talk. Aren't you? Yes, I am too. I certainly am. I'm looking forward to working with you. And don't feel alone, because you're not. I will be with you every step of the way, and I will be watching everything you do, every day from now on, so there's nothing to worry about, OK?"

People responded to statements like *I will be watching everything you do, every day from now on* in a variety of ways. There was one group, let's call them group A, or, as I like to think of them, "the Smart People." They had this conversation and immediately thought: *They track everything I do? Fuck that, I am so out of here.* And they left. They had, in HR parlance, "self-selected out," and this took care of the best and brightest, who are always the ones who cause the most problems in the long run.

Then there was group B, which ironically had a lot of type A personalities, whose members were constantly in overdrive: *I'm at 163? Not for long. I'll be 10 or 5 or 2—there can be only one! I'm kicking people out and going to the top, because I need that to get my promotion, and I need a promotion because I need to get out of here and go where they don't track everything! Look out 'cause I'll knife anybody who bugs me during my shift. I need my numbers up right now. I'll work off the clock, improve my ratings. That's it. Just five extra hours off the clock, and I'll be able to get the drop on everybody and totally get to the top.*

This happened often, which drove up the averages, and management ratcheted up the goals accordingly. Working off the clock just once was a bit like smoking just a little crack, and management must have been delighted with the results.

The very smartest of these folks might have realized that in the end, this room was actually a gerbil cage. That's why we had pellets and water bottles and were seated together in a dank and lightless hole. Even worse, one day we'd discover this was a *watertight* gerbil cage. And on that day, management would be putting a hose in the top and water would start pouring in like a bad Batman death trap, and it would be *Rats of NIMH* time. The break room would flood, the cubicle maze would become an impromptu canal system with people left standing on their door-desks, reaching for the darkened ceiling as their Christmas lights sputtered and popped. All the gerbils of CS would be screaming and scrabbling with one voice, "Let me out! Get me a job in editorial! Anywhere! Please! Let me out, they're sending my job to India—I'll have to move to Bhopul and live on one dollar an hour! My options, my sweet options, I have to keep them!"

I think most Amazonians vacillated between the two categories: they tried to be in group A, but then got scared and needed their jobs so they became Bs for a while, and then when the grind was too great they acted like As again. A few avoided this dichotomy altogether and choose the third path. I was in category C: I cheated.

I used their love of metrics against them. Great metrics could get anything forgiven because quad leaders kept their best performers like collectors hang on to star rookie cards. Being notable in the charts was the only real career insurance.

My methods weren't bulletproof. Pperry, who had finally made it out of training to work on the floor, flagged me down one afternoon.

"Daisey! Great numbers, man!"

"Uh, thanks."

"How do you do it? I can't break a minute forty-five."

"Ah—what did I do?" *Uh-oh.*

"Seventeen seconds! Your call resolution time is seventeen seconds!"

Shit.

Perhaps the most sacred of the five numbers was the one that measured average call resolution, i.e., the amount of time it took you to complete each telephone contact. Lower was better, because that meant you were handling more calls and getting that contact rate up, which meant more customers served and less wait on the phone.

To drastically improve your average all you had to do on every third or fourth call was pick up and say, "Thank you for calling Amazon.com, can I have your order," and then immediately hang up the phone. This would give you an amazing call resolution time. I mean, you're serving the customer in five seconds, three seconds, one second—that's real efficiency.

I knew it was just a matter of time before this failed spectacularly—someone would spot-check, see the short call times on individual calls, and the jig would be up. I just didn't think I would be so incredibly stupid that it would be a public execution.

"Seriously, Mike. How do you get your numbers so low?"

I looked at him—twentysomething, receding hairline, good attitude going sour after Christmas. I was probably finished anyway, so what the hell.

"Pete, I just hang up on people."

For a second it was as if I'd said *I kill and eat dogs in my cubicle.* He just stared—this was customer service heresy of the highest order. Then his face split into a grin.

"That is *so* hardcore."

And another loyal employee falls to the Dark Side.

➤ **I think my audacity saved me,**
but only barely. I pleaded login errors and technical problems
to Samantha, excuses that were grudgingly accepted. Further
errors would finish me off. It was in the sea of Fear, Uncertainty,
and Doubt that the mission statement project fell into my lap
and changed my life.

Samantha asked me to be on the mission statement project
because I had made some vague noises about wanting interaction with my fellow workers—code for "Please, please, let me
out of this department and away from these idiot phones."

Mission statements came into vogue in American business
about the time that the "Personnel" office became "Human
Resources." Filled with cheap empowerment and tacky can-do
crapola, mission statements embody the lowest form of writing imaginable. I was ecstatic about getting an opportunity to
work on one. It involved meeting with other human beings—
and, since no one has meetings with temps, this was actually
going to be my first meeting in any kind of a committee context in five years. I was stoked.

You see, it was clear to me at this point that the core of
Amazon was its public face, and the core of that public face
was Jeff. Surrounding Jeff was a cloud of aphorisms that
writhed and shifted, showing people what they wanted to see.
I wanted a chance to muck around with those slogans.

The quintessential and most popular Amazon saying is also
its most enigmatic: "It's still Day One." Although this invoca-
tion was used by Jeff on an hourly basis, it was never fully
explained because it meant a lot of different things to different
people, and Amazon liked it that way.

What it means is that it's still "Day One of the Internet," so
there are miles and miles to go in terms of growth and oppor-

tunity that will be had on the net—we haven't even begun to tap the future markets. It means it's still "Day One of Amazon's growth," so hang on—it's only going to get bigger, even if it seems like it couldn't be possible, and the company that we have now is only a seed of the future Amazon. And of course, the one that isn't spoken aloud—it's still "Day One of the stock," meaning that the promise of the fiscal future is much more lucrative than can be contained or understood. So the idea is that you didn't get in too late, because there is still so much possibility for everybody. Hence there's nothing to worry about. Stay cool. Be happy. Work hard.

Another potent interpretation had to do with the idea that Amazon was still in start-up mode. The company was not profitable, and it was clear that it might be vulnerable and unsupportable ("Amazon.bomb"), so management worked very hard to make us identify with the company and adopt a "Rebel Alliance versus the Empire" view—the rest of the world was against us and wanted us to fail, but if we worked really hard, it would happen for us. If we didn't work really hard, it wouldn't happen for us. It's the same brand of determinism used in self-empowerment seminars.

Wednesday came and I reported to the conference room to have my first grown-up meeting. There were six others in the meeting room. We played the introduction game and then listened attentively as Samantha laid out the parameters of our assignment. As I listened to what our job would be, I realized that this was one of those watershed moments of fully lucid living. Speaking vulgarly, I was getting my Amazonian cherry popped.

We were developing a mission statement not for Amazon as a company, and not for customer service—those mission statements were already written. We were being pressed into service to formulate a mission statement that would be used by our current quad. Just for the twelve people in my new quad, Route 66. The efforts to find busywork that could satisfy CSers' need for token proof that they weren't in a dead-end job had just hit a new high.

For months we debated endless variations on car metaphors that showed how "Route 66 would be in the driver's seat of Customer Service for the *Customer*!" It was unbearable but still better than being on the phones or in email an extra hour a week, and, because everyone on the committee felt the same way, it was an endless process.

The most unbearable element of the ordeal was that the Mullet served on the committee. It was like having the T-1000 as a civil service examiner.

"A point of order?"

We all shrugged, as no one knew or cared how those worked.

"Ahem. Regarding the idea floated earlier by cdawson and michaelf that we make reference in the statement to Route 66 as a 'hot rod' of service, I would refer us to the Amazon policy on discrimination. It bears noting that in its widest possible sense, which is the perspective legal professionals recommend in sensitivity issues, the use of rods or other phallic representations can be seen by some as a form of authoritarian proxy for male patterns of behavior that lead to or cause violence. While none suggest that cdawson or michaelf anticipated this interpretation, I would submit that prudence should be our byword in these matters, which is why I suggest that we consider 'fast automobile' in place of the 'heat' rod. I do hasten to add that some might suggest that reliance on automobiles as a central metaphor for the 'vehicle' of customer service does a disservice to efforts of the Green Start! program to get Amazonians to consider other methods of transport toward better ecoliving. For these reasons I also submit 'quick bus' for our consideration, though there is an unfortunate social stigma attached to public ridership that may not be in line with the public impressions Amazon wishes this statement to give. This yields my final submission of the week in this regard, the ever-obvious 'moving vehicle,' which also dodges possible questions as to how fast this metaphorical vehicle is moving, thus avoiding objections from MADD and other groups concerned with safe and courteous driving. 'Route 66 is a moving vehicle of customer service' captures the sentiments, insofar as you accept the incongruity of the base metaphor for a workgroup being transformed into conveyance."

I owe those meetings a lot. As I watched smart people waste their time week after week listening to the mind-destroying Mullet, I finally lost my last inhibitions. It was time to end this, either by moving up or crashing out. Fudging metrics wasn't enough. I set about plotting and scheming, carving my gun from a piece of soap. The movie was *Escape from Alcatraz,* and if they caught you making a break for it, you'd wish they'd killed you.

10

Interviews

My first idea for sneaking out of customer service was to look for a position in editorial. I was enchanted with the idea of writing reviews for the site. I liked the idea of being in publishing, that in one fell swoop I would be as sexy as an assistant editor at *Harper's* or *Maxim* and then hold my head up high at Manhattan parties by telling people I edited for a living. That sounded like the height of literary chichi.

While busy sucking up to a number of editors at parties and through friends of friends I observed that they were wan, drawn, and distracted. Many had facial tics and would wave their hands in front of their faces at random times in response to unknown stimuli. They looked as overworked as the CS people, although at the time that hardly seemed possible to me.

I soon learned differently. I managed to secure a side gig reviewing products, which meant that when I got home from my day in CS I had to go through bags of toys. To persuade editorial to give me this chance, I had passed myself off as a former high school educator. Thus I was given the job of evaluating and reviewing preschool children's toys. One of my reviews is included for your consideration below:

Product: Fisher-Price ABC Desk

Review: This desk set for children over eighteen months features a bright case with Elmo and Cookie Monster on the cover above a grid which can be filled with one of the many removable sheets that are printed with words. Within the clamshell case are 26 double-sided tiles, with numbers on their backs and all the letters of the alphabet on their fronts. Each letter features a familiar Sesame Street character holding an object that begins with the same letter. This allows children to become familiar with the shape of different letters, and as they become comfortable with this the set helps to show how letters form complete words. This set does a good job of reinforcing recognition, and is an excellent learning tool for children up to about three years; beyond this age most children will become disenchanted with the desk. The case itself is difficult to close with

the tiles inside, and the many one and a half inch
square tiles can quickly get underfoot.
                                            —Michael Daisey

In reality I haven't the faintest idea what this toy desk is good
for, aside from being more complete and better built than my
door-desk at work. Mix common sense ("Toy should not be
eaten") with warm pronouncements that inspire confidence
that the child will become brilliant ("The ball improves hand-
eye coordination and spatial understanding—soon your child
will understand advanced calculus") and you have written your
own toy review. It appeared that even if you had only *seen* a
child but could describe him ("like a midget with less hair"),
Amazon would let you freelance as a child-education expert.

It was fun receiving toys but it rapidly got out of hand. Due
to massive understaffing, an enormous amount of toys would
be sent each week to everyone who had signed on to do
reviews. You could beg them to slow down or stop, but to no
avail—somebody had some quotas to meet somewhere. Very
soon I was thirty, forty, fifty reviews in the hole. Our closets
were filled with Queen Amidala Star Cruisers, BioBorgs!, and
enough children's construction tools to build the Hoover Dam
out of alphabet blocks. I couldn't say no, and so they kept on
coming like a terrible Weeble Wobble Bataan Death March
Playset.

Toy reviewing is an example of something that doesn't scale
well at all. Amazon boasts of ten million items in the catalog—
reviewing even a hundredth of these would be a Herculean
task. Editorial was a plusher gerbil cage with chrome acces-
sories, but a gerbil cage nevertheless. No customers to talk to
was a plus, but having to review endless streams of Color Me
Elmo playsets and Snoopy Play Urinals slowly boiled my brain
into a thick, meaty paste.

So I procrastinated, which I am very good at, and soon the review supervisors were calling me, agitated. I pleaded with them, acted contrite, and still did nothing about the boxes that now filled up every closet and most of our living room. Then the people who needed to collect the already reviewed toys to send them back to the companies began calling me, also agitated. I begged off and asked them to please give me more time. Eventually I started ignoring them as well, right about the time a case of Beanie Babies had taken command of the kitchen.

This all came to a head one Saturday morning when a temp from Amazon drove over to my apartment to get the toys. I was inside and saw him as he walked up to the front door—and he saw me. I ran into our bedroom where Jean-Michele was writing.

"Hide! Hide!"

"What is it?"

"It's the toy people from Amazon! They want the toys!"

My Jean-Michele and I are cut from the same cloth, so instead of confronting the man or dealing with the situation, we both dove under the covers and hid in the bed. The terrible toy-recovering temp was trying our buzzer and we held our breath, waiting for him to depart.

Jean-Michele tried to calm me. "He'll go soon."

"No, he made me."

"He *made* you?"

"You know, like on cop shows. I mean he *saw* me."

"You mean he knows you're in here? Oh no oh no oh no." She sounded panicked. This wasn't going to be pretty. I should say something to inspire confidence.

"I was naked."

"Jesus Christ, Michael. You have to stop working naked by the fucking window."

"I know."

"Well." She peeked her head over the covers. "He seems to be gone."

Then, like a bad horror movie, we heard the knocking . . . no longer at the outer door, but at the door of our own apartment! We dove back under the covers.

"Shit! The building door must have been open!"

We could hear him now, right outside our door, calling loudly and repetitively, "Amazon . . . Amazon . . . Amazon here. I'm here to get the toys. Amazon." He sounded like some kind of angry zombie.

"He has to give up, right?" I didn't sound convincing.

"I don't know."

"I mean, he's a temp. What's he going to do?"

We found out what the angry zombie temp could do. From our bedroom I could see the door to our apartment shake in its hinges as the enraged temp went crazy and began to beat upon it.

"AMAZON! AMAZON! I'M HERE TO GET THE TOYS! AMAZON! I KNOW YOU ARE IN THERE! COME OUT! AMAZON!"

"Holy shit!"

"What are we going to do?"

"I don't know—this isn't right."

"AMAZON!"

"Should we open the door?" I offered.

"No! He'll know we're in here then! What are we going to do, pretend we were asleep?"

"AMAZON! COME OUT!"

"He's going to break our door!"

"Omigod, I think he will . . . should we . . ."

"COME OUT!"

"Let's just hide. Let's lie still."

Jean-Michele was right. After a few more minutes of pounding, the angry zombie temp stalked out of the building, taking with him any remaining hope or desire I'd ever had to be in editorial. No one ever contacted me again about the toys or followed up on the fifty-odd reviews I never submitted. I auctioned off the Beanie Babies at Amazon.com, where delighted collectors got to bid on each of the fourteen Snuggles the Cats™ I had been keeping in my breadbox.

With the demise of my hopes for editorial, I threw all my efforts into working my connections. Well, *connection,* singular: I knew someone who knew someone who was in a department where they were looking to expand. I smiled and she put my name in, which got me an interview—the opening I needed.

➤ When you apply for an internal

transfer within any dot-com or tech company, you enter an arcane and mysterious zone from which there is no easy egress. I blame Microsoft for this, but I don't have any evidence—I just assume the bad ideas always start with them. In any case, sometime in the last few years the interviewing process changed from a bureaucratic routine to something New Agey, torturous, and as bizarre as electing the Pope.

Maybe I'm alone in this but I seem to remember a more conventional process involving frank discussion, some handshaking and evaluation of your capabilities, mixed with some gut-level guesses about your character. That was all out at Amazon—the warm glow of team building and hyperdarwinism demanded that every applicant get a thorough scrubbing down, so you could not only know him but prove to those around you that your thoroughness was preventing the spread of mediocrity.

My internal interviews took over eight hours and involved

more than ten people—enough for an intramural rugby game. I never saw some of these people again. After I spoke to them on that day they went back to wherever they came from, perhaps some special HR department of interviewing that participates in obscene, darker activities.

I don't know how they decided things. Maybe they played rugby with the understanding that if shirts won I would get the job, and if skins won they would kick me back into the gerbil cage. I don't know, I'll never know. I do know that I have never been as flustered in an interview as I was when I tried to wrap myself around the endless whorls and loops of conversation that their questions solicited. It was like dealing with wired Jesuits who have just discovered peyote in the Communion wine. It was not only the questions they asked, but the seizure-inducing way in which they asked them.

How has customer service challenged you?

Writing a lot of email challenged me. I mean, I feel that I have a facility for applying myself to problems and issues, proactively, and then engaging policy in a way that solves problems, retroactively. Pro- or retroactively I feel that I was challenged to anticipate and respond to issues that arose, and then to . . . ah . . . analyze my responses later, and thereby know the full scope of my own actions in those situations.

Describe your greatest fear.

I have this dream where snakes are crawling up inside my body, which is an intensely Freudian image I'm not at all comfortable with. I also often dream about using a giant syringe to remove fat from my body, which is sickeningly pleasurable in a masochistic fashion, but whether that's a body-image issue or some kind of penetration-oriented phobia isn't clear.

Who would win in a fight:a lowland silverback gorilla or a Canadian grizzly bear?

The bear wins if equipped with a ranged weapon.

Describe the most beautiful thing you've ever seen.

I was in Prague, and I was walking on the Charles Bridge on an exceptionally clear night. It was early winter, and the brisk chill in the air put color into the cheeks of the winsome young girls who passed by me. A man was playing wineglasses, licking his fingers and rubbing the glass rims to make the crystal hum and sing. I had just fallen in love with my girl and she was on my arm. Her name was Jean-Michele, and we were talking about having children, which thrilled and horrified me.

You are trapped in the Arctic with an old Inuit, a pack of matches, a blanket, and a machete. Night is falling. What do you do first?

Wrestle the Inuit. In life-or-death situations, much like e-commerce, it's important to establish dominance quickly or anarchy results. Old Inuits can still be fierce combatants, so I would be wary as I incapacitated him quickly and without permanent harm. Then I'd cut the blanket into strips with the machete, smear these with the requisite seal blubber Inuits carry, and then set those aflame with the matches. The resulting flares would then be seen by rescue choppers.

What kind of dog would you be?

Pekingese. Small, compact, fierce, and finely tuned—with a small dog you get more value per pound, and if you should need to transport the dog you can keep it in your briefcase if you equip it with a small air canister and dog-shaped scuba mask. Dogs love that. They think they're astronauts.

Give an example of a low-hanging fruit you would gather.

. . . Um. Not bananas—they're high fruit. Ah . . . [*realizing error*] . . . oh. Yes. Low-hanging fruit. Well, that would be "fruit" which is "hung low" by the standards of the net—I think I'd be most concerned not with *which* fruit we gathered, but instead with the whole process of gathering as a holistic system. Amazon is a corporation with many systems and processes, and it would be wise to examine these closely, winnowing the "bad fruit" from the "good." To extend the metaphor, if I may: If Amazon wants to be the world's apple pie, only a mixture of different fruit is going to make that possible . . . [*realizing error*] . . . that is, if by "apple pie" we mean "pie of many fruits." Yes.

But you know, what they don't tell you is that you don't even have to talk in complete sentences. It's an endurance race—so long as you keep talking, you win. And I did. *I won.*

The hand of God or Jeff Bezos reached down and lifted me up out of my rat warren in the Securities Building and carried me across the great city of Seattle, all the way up to the mansion on the hill—the Fortress of Solitude where I would take my place in the business development department and receive my union card for the New Economy.

It was amazing. It was like winning the lottery. Msmith told me I was a lucky bastard who deserved to be shot. I never saw pperry on the job again. Warren warned me that the people up there wouldn't be like normal folks—they were living close to the radiance of Jeff Himself, and that may have changed them in ways we could scarcely imagine.

To: jeff@amazon.com
From: mdaisey@amazon.com
Subject: to tell you

I managed to get a position with business development. I'm not certain what I'll be doing, but at this
point I think I'd take a transfer into professional
floor licking so long as I won't ever have to answer
customer questions again.

I'm actually writing you because I have a confession to make, and you seem to be the best person to
hear it. I wrote a report to get myself promoted
out of customer service--I tracked our competitors'
customer service response times by sending them
emails and then graphing the speed of response versus the quality of their answers. Charts, graphs,
tables--I used our own metrics measurements to
focus on other companies.

I had to do it. Without something outside the system, I'd never get out on the strength of my numbers
alone. I needed something to talk about in transfer
interviews that was better than my typing speed--I
wanted to do something that would help get me
noticed. If I followed protocol I'd have never even
gotten the chance to apply.

Well it's fake--the whole thing is fake. The data,
the studies, the people I claimed to have inter-

viewed...I didn't do any of it, I was way too busy. The opportunity came, and in a flash I faked it all --thirty pages of graphs, charts, and PowerPoint presentations that boil away into ethereal bullshit, perfect sentences about absolutely nothing.

But what a piece of nothing! I have to admit I've fallen in love with my fiction--it's Russian in scope, with fearful passages, dangerous predictions, and dire warnings. I talk about the study I didn't perform as though it were my firstborn, and I'm proud of what I've created, even if it's hollow to the core.

When did this start for you? Before the bright magnification of a billion people's attention there was this independent bookstore that happened to be on the net. And it was a really cool thing.

Was there a moment when you doubted? At the first meeting with the venture capitalists? Earlier? Did you see what you had started and become just a little afraid, as I'm afraid now, that if enough people all lie at the same time we might shake the earth from her orbit?

No. Not you. You're like me. You wanted to make history.

It's intoxicating. I think about getting more options and what that might mean for me. I could retire from the office world. Open my own theater.

Subject:to tell you

Start a family. Buy a house. Simple dreams that seem so enormous they take my breath away. I could do so much good if I had enough power.

That's why I'm helping you. With this report I've added my own small stone to the top of a huge wall, and I'm so desperate to be part of something you're building that I will not look down. I know that I can do the work. Let me work. Please, let me work.

md

11

Supervillain Lair

Lex Luthor's Freak House on the Hill, a.k.a. Amazon.com Corporate World Headquarters: it squats like an art deco toad over the city of Seattle, its insides all scooped out and replaced with IKEA and geek central—a trifecta of Batcave, Fortress of Solitude, and supervillain lair. These days it's dolled up in tech-chic architecture, an ubiquitous landscape of green plate glass, thin silver wires, and exposed ductwork. I don't know what it is about tech companies and exposed ductwork—they *love* the stuff. It's as though the building's guts reflect an inner anxiety writ large, so that at any point in the day any of us can look up at the exposed piping and exclaim, "We're so busy, look how hard we're working . . . oh God, please, we're almost profitable, we're working so hard that we don't have time to cover up these ducts! They had to be left exposed! That's how dedicated we are!"

This was once the Pacific Medical Center, built between world wars to care for shell-shocked soldiers coming home. Despite the zealous retrofit, it feels like a hospital even now, and I think that this cannot be an accident—the spin doctors who labor here are too clever to have let that slip by.

It was within these hallowed halls that everything changed for me. They had these things they called "windows" that looked out on "sunlight," and if you opened the windows then this air called "wind" would come in . . . it was sweet. I had a cube, my own cube with walls that went up high, lots of room, and a chair for visitors—it was a swank cube. Very badass. No one tried to bunk with me—all mine! I sat in my cube for hours with my arms outstretched, enjoying the silence and space.

It was a brave new world and I gave thanks every day that I was part of it. It took some getting used to—not the pace or the Amazon devotional prayers at noontime—but the shift in social status. Going from CS to the Mansion on the Hill was a lot like an enlisted man making good; I had a lot more status than I used to, but I wasn't allowed to forget where I had come from.

People did things differently. No one kept track of when you came in or left, which was fine since mostly people didn't leave. Since we were up on a hill away from downtown, they built a cafeteria in the building that served up fare that tasted remarkably like Chicken Orzo Salad with Almond Slivers and Poppy Seed Dressing. People would come and give you massages, pick up your personal mail, clean up your waste, and do your laundry while you waited. And of course, if you needed a book, CD, DVD, electronic organizer, rocking chair, table saw, or antique cedar chest, you could order it from Amazon and they would bring it to your office. You simply can't imagine how addictive Amazon is when you can 1-Click™ and anything you desire shows up in your cube a few hours later. Combined with my increased salary it was like living in those mining towns where you buy everything on credit from the company store, except instead of hooch and hookers we'd spend our credit on John McPhee anthologies and Puccini boxed sets.

And there were dogs, dogs, dogs everywhere! Jeff had this huge hard-on for dogs. That love had been transmitted into the DNA of the company, which made it compulsory for all of us to be dog people as well. So Jeff had it written into the lease for the Fortress of Solitude that dogs would be allowed on all the floors. They panted and barked and padded their way all over the massive castle, and everyone had to have one since this was one of the most awesome perks of working at Amazon—you could bring your dog with you! Left unspoken was the fact that you had to—otherwise the dogs would starve to death at home, waiting for their masters to show up on weekends and feed them. It's standard dot-com operating procedure: give your employees a video game machine, a foosball table, or let them bring their dogs, and they will live at their desks, plugged in and working, because they have everything they can think of right there. Why leave? You'll be coming back tomorrow anyway.

Like so many corporate enclaves, Amazon made it more and more attractive to just stay there rather than drive back to the paltry furnishings of your apartment or house. There were rumors that you could get a bonus if you volunteered to give up your place of residence and just hang your hat in your cubicle, but except for the programmers, that was probably just talk.

The best thing about the dogs was that nobody put them on leashes because this was Seattle and that would have been so oppressive, so they roamed up and down the hallways in packs. No joke—there were packs of dogs, all shapes and sizes, wandering up and down the spooky, echoing halls. When you stepped out of the elevator they turned toward you, jogged down the hallway lolling their hungry tongues, tried to ride up and down to other floors, took over stairwells. Wild dogs on every floor—everyone would have been scared if they were Hispanics, but they're not, they're just dogs, so it's fine! I subscribed to the dogs@amazon.com email list even though I didn't own one.

At Amazon we were obsessed with "scaling": the idea that solutions to problems must not only work now, but keep working as you double or triple the size of the system. In the dot-com world, demand could grow like a virus, so you needed to keep it tight: multiply current customers by ten or a hundred and the system still had to require the same number of Amazon employees to keep the machine running. You have to plan your business this way if you build everything around the assumption that you have an infinite customer base. And we knew that in order to keep Amazon's stock value increasing at 1998 speed, we would need to have ten trillion customers by 2015, so to ensure we could serve them all we had to ignore logic (Where were these people going to come from, Alpha Centauri?) and concentrate on solving this insoluble logistics problem. I would discover in business development that a reference to "scaling" made for a great ad hoc response to any issue, if said with a slightly arched eyebrow and one thumb hooked into a belt loop of your khakis:

"Yes, interesting . . . but does it *scale*?"

"Vertically speaking, moving forward, this solution must be able to scale logarithmically to mode increased customer throughput."

"Could you scale my Value Meal?"

The greatest social change had to do with the way the stock was handled. Up on the hill it was a totally different ballgame—the respectful silence of the underlings was out the window. While publicly yakking about your specific compensation package was verboten, the sky was pretty much the limit otherwise. When the stock dipped we all chatted. When it rose we chatted. When it remained stable we chatted even more, wondering a bit fearfully if it had finally reached a plateau. I don't remember a lot of concern that the price would drop permanently—apparently we believed the worst thing that could happen to a stock was that it would remain level and not grow by leaps and bounds, tying us down like some company with "profits" and "stores" like Kmart.

It went so far that everyone in my new department had DayTech Online macroed onto F3, for day-trading stocks at their desks. I asked them about it.

"It kicks ass—I made sixty grand last year on the side."

"Really?"

"Yeah . . . Real Networks, I bought low and used the margin—you can really make a killing here. Made up for some other trades, still came out on top."

"Ah . . . wow. That's a lot of money." I am the comeback master.

"Yep. You should start trading, Daisey."

"Isn't it kind of risky?" I had always been skittish about stock trading, which is ironic when you consider that I had staked my future on the value of Amazon's stock, which made me the ultimate high-risk investor.

Supervillain Lair

"Sure, but life is risk. The trick is to have enough resources so you can play the whole field, covering your shorts by keeping an eye on stocks where you want to play the margin long, so you *bzzzz* stock *bzzzz bzzz bzzzzzzzz,*" and the person would drone on about their personal flavor of invincible bull-market investing, eventually coming around to " . . . and of course, you're a smart guy—you won't have trouble. There's money waiting to be taken."

That was the consensus: money was waiting to be taken, as if money were a very cute girl with a great personality whom no one had thought to ask to the prom. If you just had some initiative and a decent car, bam, you were in your own John Hughes movie.

Maybe the fact that people all around us had cashed out some of this stock and were enjoying their wealth just made us more bold. Due to Jeff's hyperdarwinism all the people being hired now were MBAs and ultracompetent; you would look at them and know that they beat out sixty people for their position, and they would smile dazzlingly, go snowboarding, and drink purified mountain water. They *sweated* purified mountain water. They checked their email using thought alone, moved things with their minds—seriously next-level shit.

Our meetings always began with stock picks. My new colleagues would turn to me and ask, "What about you, Mike? Cisco or Yahoo!?" Knowing nothing about stocks, I would find myself saying, "Buy Planet Hollywood," because I had heard they were going bankrupt and wanted to make everyone laugh. And they did laugh, and they moved on to the next guy, and I hacked out a place for myself in the social order.

Not everyone I worked with was hip or cutting edge, but almost all of them had spiky hair and leather pants, as well as great cars and expensive things. They looked so generically cool that I found myself wondering constantly, "Who are these people?" They weren't mainstream enough to be yuppies, nor were they at all alternative, even if a bunch of them dressed that way—so who the fuck were these people I wanted to be?

And one day I met a new guy in our department with a great smile and fine bone structure who shook my hand firmly. He remembered me from college and suddenly I realized the answer. All those Delta Taus and PoliSci majors at my microivy—I never knew what happened to them. Business development was where they ended up, each and every one of them, a string of middle- and upper-management frat boys and sorority sisters massaging the American Dream.

Let's be clear, though—I loved my position. In fact, I longed to be closer to the people around me. Nine months of Amazonian conditioning had convinced me that I had been blindingly wrong ever to want to strike out on my own. I had never made more than a subsistence-level income before, scratching out terrible day jobs while I worked on theatrical projects and comedy and whatever other non-income-generating hobbies I liked. I had accepted this inevitability, in part because I felt there was no alternative—I didn't know what I could do to make money, so I had never sold out. But once I had Amazon, my nonpaying arts became less and less real. No one could survive by doing what they wanted, I told myself . . . I remembered my old lifestyle nostalgically, a youthful indulgence of time that could have been better spent. A diversion before my *real* work began, like boomers who recall the sixties with relish as they balance their money-market accounts. Did I really want to go around exposing myself to children in grotesque French dramas? The answer was obvious.

Here, with these sexy people, working at the center of the digital world atop this massive hill—this was so much more quantifiable and nakedly impressive. I was anxious to sell out, now that it would be worth something. I was at the front of the line. What had liberal arts and crowing at the moon ever done for me before? Now I was with my long lost brothers and sisters, Delta Taus and PoliScis one and all, and I loved all of them—I return, the prodigal son! I was the Aesthetics guy—who knew I would be reunited with all of them on this prosperous, upwardly mobile path? I was in love with a beautiful woman; I had the respect of her family and my family and the world; I could trade stock at my desk; I had a window with sunlight; I was a low-key, modest, fully wired Dilettante of the Universe. It was the happiest time of my life.

➤ On gray Sunday afternoons Jean-Michele and I were often at Starbucks, staring out the window back at the world. Nowhere to be, nothing to do but drink his and hers vanilla lattes: mine grande and hers tall. She used to get hers short, but Starbucks had instigated a national supersizing campaign—you needed to argue aggressively with them to get anything smaller than tall, and in a few short years it was clear the available sizes would be huge, mega, and el café enormoso. God bless America—we can't get universal health care, but *damn* if these aren't some gigantic coffees.

"Do you want to go to the picnic this year?"

"Christ, is it that time again?"

I nodded. "It is. The guys in BizDev are putting a broomball team together."

"Broomball?"

"Yeah, broomball. It's that game we play every year, with the soccer ball and the brooms, remember?"

"Yes." Her brow furrowed petitely. "Wasn't that the game where people broke their bones and the ambulances came to take them away?"

"Well, only two people, but yes."

"And you smear war paint on your faces?" Jeff had sported really fetching blue and yellow stripes, like Woody Allen playing a cameo in *Braveheart*.

"That's the fun part."

"Uh-huh." She sipped. "No, I don't think so." Another sip. "I have an especially large employee orientation tomorrow and then the rest of the week is open enrollment for benefits." Jean-Michele had given up on the student thing and had become an employment assistant for a local hospital's human resources department. "If it's really important to you I can go, but after next week I think I'll just want to sleep."

"I understand," I said, and I did understand. When we hadn't been looking, sleep had become the most valued drug in our life, harder to score than pot or ecstasy.

Jean-Michele put her coffee down and leaned forward. "Michael, are you scared?"

"Of getting married?"

She nodded. I sipped my coffee, which is a bad move when you're asked an important question.

"I know I should be terrified, but I'm not."

She looked relieved. "Me too."

I wanted to say something important, but instead I said, "We're doing really well now."

"It's amazing. I never thought we'd get here."

"I suppose we'll be able to buy a house in a year or two, knock on wood." I rapped twice on the softly burnished beech-veneer pressboard table.

"Do you want a house?"

"I don't know," I said quietly. "What about you?"

"I guess so. It would be a great investment."

"I *do* know I want to marry you. Everything else I don't know, but I do know that."

She smiled suddenly at that and the room warmed. She laid her hand on my arm, lightly, barely brushing my skin with her fingertips—I remember that one sensation more clearly than anything else that year.

"It is so good to be here with you today," she said. We sat there in the Starbucks like every Starbucks from Cape Cod to Beijing, enjoying the climate control and the overstuffed chairs, basking in the cool white reading light, reading the corporate coffee haikus off the walls out loud to each other all afternoon.

12

Pornsniffing

Six-thirty A.M. in the Fortress of Solitude. I was seated in the cafeteria watching light and rain spill over the downtown of Seattle at the same time. I picked at my food. Seated across from me was Cody, my constant breakfast companion. The cafeteria was empty—the Filipino minimum-wageslaves had only just started serving, and the hordes of nibbling dot-commers hadn't made it to work yet. Cody and I liked to start early; later, when we left at six or seven, we'd feel more entitled to get out of the office.

In the interest of full disclosure, there was no one named Cody there with me—I never had a coworker named Cody. Cody is a composite of four or five coworkers melded and compressed into one breathing body. Picture this composite as male, industrious, sardonic, white, slightly overweight, and well-meaning. He paid his taxes on time, wanted to marry a girl he'd been living with for a few years, just made a down payment on a pretty swank house, and flossed. Cody wore khakis, a smart belt, sensible shoes, and a blue shirt whose hue varied according to his mood the way some lizards change skin shades, from pale blue (excited) to cornflower blue (less excited) to velvety blue (barely excited).

"Daisey, did you go to Catch's party this weekend?"

"No."

"Me neither."

"It sounded like it was going to be pretty epic."

"Well, it *is* Catch we're talking about."

Catch worked with us in BizDev—he was the kind of guy that epitomized BizDev, and who then went on to popularize the use of other contractions like HuRe for Human Resources, SitRep for Situation Report, and MaCaBroDo for My Car Has Broken Down. He did a thing I had previously seen only in movies, where somebody makes their hand into a gun, points it at you, and pretends to shoot while saying "Gotcha! Catch ya later!"

Everybody loved Catch—he was an attention magnet. More important, he was genuinely unguarded, a rarity in corporate, friendly, and just a little bit goofy. The gun thing was grating, but amazingly you could get used to it. Catch is not a composite—Catch is real.

"He was predicting about three hundred people."

"Damn." Catch's digs did make for a great party space, and Catch seemed to know absolutely everyone from everywhere—three hundred wasn't out of the question. It was like a college dream of what parties could be, given unlimited fake IDs, no social anxiety, and bottomless tequila shooters. I thought about a three-hundred-person Catch-fueled party and what cleanup after that might look like. It looked like another problem that wouldn't scale—I recalled my freshman dorm on Sunday mornings, multiplied it tenfold, and then gave up. I could see the carpet of Cool Ranch Doritos gently sautéing in warm, spilled microbrew.

Catch lived a documentary-ready version of the dot-com dream. He rented an entire floor of some abandoned factory in Seattle's Historic Pioneer Square, a massive space whose industrial history and dark, foreboding architecture made it absurdly expensive. The tech culture had fallen in love with abandoned places. I think that comes from movies, where the Geek Sidekick to the hero has a secret lab/weapons facility downtown by the docks—it looks like a moldy warehouse, but it's fully wired and filled with Beowulf clusters, heat-seeking bullets, and Kevlar underwear. You may not have had enough scratch to build a Fortress of Solitude, but that didn't stop you from trying.

He looked the part: tall, standard-issue blond spiky hair and leather pants, as well as a great big dog with an enormous amount of character. The last went a long way at Amazon corporate, where dog choice could play a large role in your future.

"Yeah, I just didn't think I could handle it. I don't know how he does all that stuff and manages to get himself into work."

"Dog does it," I said.

"What?"

"Really. He fans business proposals out in front of Dog and whichever ones Dog puts his paw on are the ones that he follows up on."

Catch's dog, named Dog, was a large husky with bat ears and some sort of breathing problem that made him lethargic. He would lie on his side in the middle of our department, looking existentially forlorn and so utterly immovable that delegations from AOL and hotcompanyoftheweek.com would have to detour around his body. When Dog started howling, which happened periodically, Catch would howl back. They made a winning combination.

"That's bullshit."

"Swear to God."

"Daisey, that is so entirely stupid."

"Hey, it's not my system."

"Yes, it is, since you are the one fucking making up this shit."

That was true. As far as I knew, Dog was not yet playing a role in Amazon policy decisions. But unlike Cody, I didn't think that the day was far off—BizDev was having as many problems scaling as the rest of Amazon. The workforce kept increasing quickly, and the workload was doubling every few months as Amazon took on new markets like home furniture, cut-rate dentistry, and third world crop irrigation. The geometry of triage was becoming more and more one-sided, leaving no time to pursue good and bad ideas alike. Eventually we would be forced to give Dog a chance.

Catch had ostensibly leased the space as part of a business he planned to start on the side, a startling ambition given the all-consuming nature of our work. His was one of the more plausible business plans I heard in BizDev—his loft's abandoned factory floor was to become the world headquarters of a website featuring all-natural organic dog food made with local microbrewed beer. Presumably, the dogs would love the taste of quality beer as much as humans do, which seems a safe bet as dogs love everything, and then the cash would roll in on this low-overhead, beer-and-meat-mixing carnival ride to riches.

It was a fine idea for a mom-and-pop operation, but the crazy part was that on weekends he'd fly to Florida, where he'd go to gigantic pool parties with dot-com players and venture capitalists who were always just a few steps away from giving him a hideous amount of money. In any other age this would have been unbelievable, but since he worked at Amazon and had gotten in early they listened to everything he said. Amazon was the stamp of success in those days—anyone from stock boy to cafeteria worker could hold forth on the future of e-commerce and people would actually listen. I don't think Catch was that serious about the company—it was a hobby—but the lure of possible riches for the flimsiest of reasons kept him in the game. Many people would be interested in $4 million for cooking dog food and beer.

"How's your CueCAT project going?"

"Oh, good. I heard back from them yesterday. You know, the scary thing is when I talk to them, I think they believe their own bullshit."

"Those poor bastards."

One of the perks of being in BizDev was that even though I was a peon and had peon duties, I could throw around the name of my department and make waves. I had used my dubious credentials to get in touch with someone at the company who was making the CueCAT, because I had read about it and wanted to know what kind of crack the company was smoking.

"How's it going to work?"

"Well, they're going to give away all these optical scanners that are hand-sized, that you can plug into a PC, right? So you have to plug in this hardware, *and* you need to install a driver from a CD. And then, their logic goes, you'll be reading a magazine and see an interesting advertisement."

"Oh yes, that happens to me often!"

"Right. So you are captivated by this interesting ad, and you think, *Gosh, I wonder whether there is any more information on this company or this product I am looking at?*"

"So you type in the name of their website—"

"No—that would be the old-school way. This is where the CueCAT comes in! Instead, you bring the magazine over to the computer and use the CueCAT's scanner to scan a bar code . . . and then you'll be automatically taken to . . ."

"The website?"

"Bingo."

"Wow. That sounds a lot harder than typing victorias-secret.com."

"The best part is that after the guy is done pitching it to me, I ask him really politely why this is easier than typing in the URL and he just starts to self-destruct. It's as if no one ever asked him that before. You could hear him crumbling on the phone."

"Weird."

"It can also scan the bar codes on food, tell you what it is."

"Eh. I can *look* at my food and know what it is."

"But wait—the scanner is going to be shaped like a cat."

"No!"

"Yeah—hence CueCAT. It'll be this little beige plastic cat."

"That will help immensely. Do they have backing?"

"Are you kidding? They have thirty million dollars."

"That's a lot of cat food."

We loved dishing over companies with stupid business plans, bizarre products no one needed, and websites that could never make a dime. We never thought of ourselves as being in the same category as iVillage, Boo.com, or Pseudo—we were Amazon.com, the grandfather and overlord, above reproach. Even if it was hard to explain to others how we were going to become profitable and justify the stock valuation, we certainly weren't running around willy-nilly throwing money in the toilet like yahoos. No free soda here, and our desks were made out of doors, for God's sake—that had to mean we were more sensible.

I asked Cody, "Have you talked with Employee #5 lately?"

"*Talked with?* Is that a joke?"

"He hasn't spoken to me in a couple of weeks."

"He's mad at life. You have some reason to think it's personal?"

My manager was Employee #5—that is to say he was the fifth employee ever hired at Amazon.com. Your employee number was a key factor in establishing your pedigree: the lower the number, the closer you were to Jeff and to the mystical early days. Mine was in the low three digits, which was a world away from 5. Five! In Amazonian terms it was like working with someone who was living history, whom we should encase in Plexiglas and keep in the lobby across from the bear with the gigantic penis.

He was the fifth employee at Amazon.com, he was still working there, and he was depressed. Very, very depressed—the kind of depression that comes off in black waves. He was a large guy, looking for all the world like a bulky wolf in his office, staring balefully into his monitor. A bulky, depressed wolf who'd been working at Amazon.com for thirty or forty dog years, which when combined with his late-forties physical age made him ancient before his time.

I had trouble wrapping my mind around the idea that someone could be so depressed and yet be worth $300 million. I am clear that money does not *actually* buy happiness, but still . . . I kept thinking that a certain amount of it, say $300 million, must make you a little less terminally depressed. It just seemed to follow.

But he was depressed. He didn't understand why he wasn't a

vice president. Why hadn't he risen as far as other people? What was wrong with him? Amazon had not been as kind to him as it had been to others who had come in as early as he had, and he wanted to know why.

You have to understand that things were very different in the early days. In those heady first days of 1,000 percent annual growth there wasn't time to work out promotions. It was a matter of seeing someone you had smoked a bowl with once and saying, "Hey! Hey, you, over there! Yeah, you, put down that box. Yeah, yeah, you're a manager now, yeah, your group's over there . . . yeah—go manage those people and, uh, we're gonna get something for you to work on soon or something, yeah, yeah, get big fast, good luck." And chances are that was the last clear directive you would ever be given, since all the people who promoted you would be promoted themselves about twenty seconds later into five different product categories.

So times changed, and Employee #5 was left behind rather than heading up the infinitely up-and-to-the-right promotion track at Amazon. He couldn't understand where things had gone wrong. He believed he was a sharp programmer and excellent innovator, and he was right on both those counts: he was the smartest person I've ever had as a supervisor by an order of magnitude. He could solve problems by looking at them. On a whim he had come up with website referrals, the idea that a website could link to Amazon and then get a small cut of each item bought by customers it referred—a tossed-off notion that spawned an entire industry.

The reason he was left behind was that he had absolutely no social graces. He could not even look people in the eye. That's not to say that he didn't confront people—he did, with extreme prejudice, telling subordinates and coworkers exactly why their ideas would fail with excruciating color commentary and total clarity. HR weenies would put these behaviors on the "Not Good Traits for a Manager" checklist.

It all came down to legacy. You see, Employee #5 had been trained as an old-school serious UNIX programmer. That's what he had originally been hired for before he had been plunged into management. Of the varied species of IT creatures you can encounter, UNIX programmers are the most ornery, reclusive, and least likely to possess skill sets appropriate for management. Communicating in the UNIX language is pretty much the opposite of human interaction: you type commands at the prompt and the box does exactly what you tell it to immediately. Bringing those traits over to the management arena wasn't such a hot idea. Sharp guy, bad manager.

It also became increasingly clear that he was simply waiting out his five-year term in order to collect on his stock options. Who could blame him? They must have been worth at least $50 million more. At the same time, the pace of Amazon, for which he had suffered on the front lines longer than almost anyone else, had taken its toll, and without the golden handcuffs he would have walked away earlier—he had $300 million—but how could you leave behind $50 million? He had a script written on the system so that at a prompt he could type:

```
[cs-styx:employee5]>howlong
```

The mainframe would spit back the exact amount of time that remained before he could retire. It got to the point that any time you came to him with a problem he would say, "That is important, but could it wait"—he would type up the command with blinding speed—"eleven months, nine days, five hours, and fourteen minutes?" He was a borderline burnout, suffering from the post-traumatic stress disorder effects of four Christmases in a row.

Employee #5 was not only an old-timer, but also *the* originator of huge sections of Amazon's underlying system—legend had it that he'd built most of the first-generation system out of cow gut and bailing wire. Word was that if he wished, he could log in, type a few commands, and send the whole system crashing down. That's why when he spent a lot of his time in his office with the door closed, people would say, "Oh, don't worry about Employee #5, he's busy. He's working on something important—leave him alone." It doesn't pay to anger a demented god or a burned-out superuser, and Employee #5 was both.

His office was near my cube and I walked by it constantly. Seeing that he always left his door open slightly, I started peeking in each time I passed. I couldn't resist. And I saw that most of the time, to my amazement, he was playing Rogue.

Rogue is sort of pre-modern-era electronic Dungeons & Dragons. There are no actual graphics; asterisks and question marks make up the walls of the maze. You walk around as a little letter *a* and you bump into the letter *b* and then on the bottom as you tap in your moves it says:

```
>>YOU HIT THE HOBGOBLIN WITH YOUR
   SWORD.
>>YOU HAVE KILLED THE HOBGOBLIN!
>>YOU FIND 12 SILVER PIECES ON THE
   HOBGOBLIN BODY.
>>CONGRATULATIONS!
```

In 1981 this had been a hard-core game, but this was 1999 and he was playing it six to eight hours a day. Except for me, no one in BizDev was a big enough geek to recognize what on earth was on his screen; they assumed it was some kind of secret project. Instead he was off killing goblins, hunting through the Mines of Moria looking for what he needed to kill in order to get the message:

```
>>YOU HIT THE BEZOS PRIME WITH YOUR
   SWORD.
>>YOU HAVE KILLED THE BEZOS PRIME!
>>YOU FIND 50 MILLION DOLLARS IN
   STOCK OPTIONS ON THE BEZOS PRIME.
>>CONGRATULATIONS!
```

I realize now that he treated all of us the same way, and I shouldn't have been so paranoid about his not looking at or speaking to me. But I'm sensitive—I thought maybe he didn't like me. I've got a great need to be accepted, so I took his behavior personally and I really wanted to find a way to make him like me. So I had a brilliant idea: I would show him my geek bona fides and talk to him about Rogue. Then he would know we had things in common and maybe a deeper respect and understanding would spring forth from this, and he would show me cool things to do with the UNIX system and I would show him newfangled games on the Sony PlayStation.

It seemed like a great plan, so that is precisely what I did: I walked into his office and just started mumbling, "Hey, it's Rogue . . . cool . . . hey, you're killing goblins . . . check that out . . . yeah . . ."

He didn't talk to me for three months. He didn't speak to me in the cafeteria, didn't speak to me at meetings, didn't respond to emails . . . I was eight feet away and yet he wouldn't acknowledge my existence. I was off the network, firewalled, shut down. In his mind his team had one less member.

Pornsniffing

"Daisey?" My composite guest
at breakfast was feeling ignored.

"Sorry—I was distracted. Just don't ever talk to him about Rogue."

"What's Rogue?"

"Exactly. Stay ignorant and remain silent."

"Daisey, you are really weird."

"I know. I don't belong here."

"I wish I could help."

"I wish you could too. God, I just wish . . . I wish that I could make lists and just *execute* them. That simple thing. I wish that I didn't scheme and scam my way from day to day. I wish I went to bed early and I wish—"

"You wish you were effective?"

"Yeah, I suppose. That would cover it."

"Well," he said, as he finally finished picking at his waffle, "since I'm just an amalgam I doubt I have a lot of pull."

"I know."

"You know, you could have given me a little more personality. Your coworkers are more interesting than you're giving me credit for."

"Eh. You're right and I'm sorry. It's just . . . how would I know? We live in this mansion on this hill and we meet day after day, see each other more than our loved ones, eat the Chicken Orzo Salad our whole lives, and I don't know even one person. Not really, not in an enduring way."

"Maybe you're not trying."

"Maybe you're right—maybe I'm not."

"You want to try more?"

"I don't know."

"Listen, everybody feels uneasy about working at Amazon. It feels like a dream, and we keep waiting to see if we'll wake up and find we have nothing. Then we think we'll never wake up and we'll all be rich or some shit like that. Most of the time I just think it'll always be like this, running and running and barely making it each quarter, hanging on to the edge for years and years. It's many things, but it's not peaceful."

"I thought you'd never say a word against Amazon."

"I'm a group consensus, not a propaganda tool. You ready to go?"

"Yeah, let's get back to work."

"I wish I was on porn duty today."

"I hear you."

→ Porn duty, a.k.a. pornsniffing, was a once-a-week routine that rotated between the folks in my department. It was necessary because sites that for PR reasons we preferred not to have linked to us would join the program. We didn't want middle America up in arms about the NAMBLA folks using Amazon.com as their store and thereby having Amazon logos up next to man/boy love photos on their website. That would be, in PR lingo, "unfortunate."

So every Tuesday somebody would cull from the database the names of URLs connected to Amazon that seemed suspicious. You'd get a list like:

a) bettycrocker.com
b) boyofsexx.org
c) mysmallandhappypuppy.net
d) nazipartyforever.tv
e) lovemelovemycouch.org
f) hotwetasiangirls.com

It is pretty short work to use key words and a little common sense to decide that checking out b, d, and f might be a good idea. When you got to hotwetasiangirls.com your job would be to inspect the site and determine just how hot and wet these Asian girls really were—were they too hot and too wet? If so, you revoked their membership and sent them a termination letter.

There were extenuating circumstances, of course: it might turn out that hotwetasiangirls.com was a site for women of Asian descent who, owing to poor circulation, had a medical need to hydrate themselves with hot liquids. More often it was a judgment call between nekkid pictures and tasteful erotic art.

I liked the job for a couple of reasons. I enjoyed having to make judgments on sites, looking over their content and issuing a thumb up or down. Who was I to judge? Well, aesthetics is defined as the philosophical study of beauty and art; it is the attempt to answer chestnuts like "What is art?" and "What is beauty?" In some ways I felt that when I was pornsniffing I was performing the only job for which my degree had ever qualified me.

To: jeff@amazon.com
From: mdaisey@amazon.com
Subject: accident

I'm writing because I can't stop replaying from this morning those magnificent doomed moments in my mind: how I brushed my arm against the counter, my attention diverted by the search for a dime (damned dime!) in my pockets, the way my left arm lost track of itself, went rogue, collided with your small frame as I stumbled through my half-turn and then it all spirals down from there--arm moving, coffee tipping, your shocked face as my hot coffee poured out on your immaculate leg.

It should never have been allowed to happen. My friend Jane once tried to give Bill Gates a five-pound bag of shredded cheese at Comdex--she was immediately escorted away and strip-searched. I'm concerned about the lack of security around your person. What if the innocent coffee I carried had instead been hydrochloric acid, or that McDonald's coffee they pressure-boil up to seven hundred degrees? You could have been needing skin grafts rather than just a new pair of khakis--this is no time to be a hero.

I'm also concerned about my own motives: why did I do this? Could my unconscious mind crave contact

with you so badly that it would resort to this bla-
tantly childish espresso-laced assault? Was it simple clumsiness, as I indicated while trying to dry
your pants in a nonhomoerotic manner? Or did the
frantic way I buffed your trousers disguise deeper
feelings that dare not speak their name?

It's true that I am experiencing a number of issues
with my employment here at Amazon and that I spend
an inordinate amount of time thinking about you and
your needs, your lifestyle, your activities. I do
not know where the line between devoted employee
and casual stalker lies, but I suspect I obliter-
ated it today.

I never hear from you, Jeff--I wish that you'd part
the curtain just the tiniest bit and let us inside.
It might weaken my resolve to concoct passive-
aggressive schemes like coffee-hurling. If I could
just get some straight information around here,
we'd all sleep better at night.

On the off chance that you'd like to tackle some
questions, here are the ones at the top of my personal list:

1) Is it true that you're building the stock up to
amass capital in order to help fund private space
exploration? Lots of people have heard this one--
it sounds crazy, but you love space, and it would
comfort many if the strategy over the years had

been a kooky master plan. Letting us believe that there's any plan at all, even a crazy one, would be a kindness.

2) If you were an analyst at D.E. Shaw again, crunching numbers for the best and the brightest, how would you rate this company you've built? You already warn small-potatoes investors not to buy the stock--what would you tell big institutions to do if you were still an analyst?

3) Why is there a fifty-thousand-year-old cave bear skeleton in the lobby with a twelve-inch penis bone? You bought it at an auction and had it placed there, but no one knows why. I really like it. When I'm here late I go and stand in front of it and think about how difficult it would be to have a bone inside of my penis, which according to Britannica Online is a fact of life for nearly all other large mammals. Score one for the humans.

md

13

Fiscal
Wonderland

All this talk about bear penises and
pornography skirts a very important
question: just what *exactly* did business
development do? Did anything work-
related ever happen at Amazon? How
could anyone have so much time for
obsessive minutiae? I'll address these
valuable questions presently.

If you work in the corporate world you have probably come into contact with those who dwell in departments with supremely bland names like Business Development, Corporate Relations, Business Relations, or Corporate Development. You may even have wondered: *Who are these people? They look well fed, manicured, effective—I wonder what it is that they are doing while I file their mail and lick their boots?* Don't be shy—it's a natural question. You may even suspect that I would be in a position to tell you what they do, seeing as how I worked in business development and if anybody was going to take the pulse of BizDev, it would be me.

I am saddened to report that you are entirely mistaken—I have no certain knowledge of what BizDev did, how it functioned, or why it came to be an institution in the first place. Despite all my time within the Inner Sanctum, I have no full understanding of how Amazon's accounting system works, how we intended to pay off our debts, why we thought this would fool anybody, or just what is in the Colonel's secret recipe. I don't know the secret plans for management to flee to Brazil. I don't know why we built seven million square feet of warehouse space that never got used—no one knows the answer to that one. The shocking truth is that when I arrived in BizDev I only understood 30 percent of the buzzwords I heard. My ignorance is large—it contains multitudes.

As an aside, it is possible that you are perusing this book in order to glean business advice, waiting for Solomon's Key to be revealed in Five Easy Pieces, which you will then use to unlock your potential and become a messianic capitalist hotshot. It is also possible that you are hungry for scraps of lore about how big bad Amazon fell down on the job, and how you, with your great smile and a much more focused e-tailing strategy, might get the job done right. If so, you bought the wrong book. Those revelations will not be occurring here. I have been informed by my editor and publishing house that if you have read all the way to this point, you have probably kept this book far too long to return it.

This is not to imply that because we didn't know where we were going we weren't *working*—to the contrary, everyone was so effective and fast-moving that to look at them made your teeth hurt. We were all doing a great deal of work and moving very quickly—I just don't know what it was that we were actually doing, moment to moment, day to day. You could walk into a colleague's office and say, "Hey, do you have a minute?" And he'd be sitting there, waving his hands in the air very quickly back and forth and he'd say, "Can't talk now—very, very busy." You'd ask slowly, "Ah . . . what are you busy doing?" To which he would naturally respond, "Moving my arms, like this, back and forth, all day long, very, very busy, good-bye."

It's easy to see how this can happen. When you work in an office everything becomes an abstraction. The higher you travel up the chain, the less actual work is being done, as everyone becomes responsible for overseeing those below them, who are supervising those below them, ad nauseam. In the Vedic tradition Hindus believe that the world's firmament rests on four elephants, who in turn stand on the back of a turtle. The question always comes: "What's holding up the turtle?" And the answer is: "It's turtles all the way down." Likewise in corporations—it is all turtles, straight to the bottom, and after a while it becomes impossible to feel what is happening at an experiential level. Only lunch meetings persist. Postmodern capitalism.

My ignorance was hardly unique—ignorance was the biggest factor clouding issues for the development of Amazon. How quickly would people get onto the net? No one knew. What customer retention rate could we expect from an online store? *Pffffft.* Which would be more important on the web: price, convenience, or customer experience? We said "all three" because there were sixteen pundits for each position and no conclusive evidence that anyone was right. It was a new frontier, and when your department is intended to forge alliances and predict what is next but you can't get solid answers to anything, you suddenly find that you're practicing voodoo. The cardinal rule at Amazon was *keep moving.* That's not bad advice—it certainly beats paralysis, which was the only alternative.

This would have worked better if the entire enterprise hadn't been fueled by stock hysteria. I can't speak for other companies, but it could be said that Amazon's business development existed to train employees to use canes to keep all the plates spinning in the air. Business development was the place where you made alliances with other companies, where you made acquisitions. It was the place where you linked to somebody else—it was like a corporate dating service or a professional lunch-eating union. It was ground zero for tweaking, prodding, and goosing the stock.

Since the entire dot-com machine was designed with massive, ever-increasing valuations *and* an absence of historical data, everyone's numbers got skewed so far over to the right that they fell off the graphs. We even had a saying that Catch used all the time: "up and to the right," meaning that whatever chart you were using had to fly up and to the right in the beautiful staircase pattern needed to sell Amazon and thus the stock.

Left unspoken was the fact that you would be forced to tweak it, change the scale, and alter the time line until you got that perfectly optimistic appearance. It was no different than being in college and changing the font of your term paper from Times New Roman 12 to Helvetica 14 in order to make a ten-page essay a thirteen-page one . . . except that fudging in college didn't normally involve millions of investor dollars.

Take best/worst/median predictions. Used by every company, this is the standard practice of modeling a number of hypotheticals to see what will happen to your business. At Amazon our numbers were so absent, and the magnetic force of positivism so necessary, that even the "worst" scenarios assumed a good economy, stock stabilization at ultrahigh levels, and a staggeringly high new-customer rate. It had to look that good, because so many assumptions went in to Amazon's existence every day that if we called all those into question our Magic 8 Ball might come up with the answer: "Close shop, flee country, beg forgiveness."

At the same time, we all wanted it to work so badly because Amazon was cool. It was cool to be able to order the *Complete Works of Dickens* at two A.M. in your skivvies. The media loved us because Jeff was a goofball and everyone fought over our destiny, which made for excellent copy. Customers loved us because at its core, Amazon was a lovely thing—it worked, it was convenient, informative, and efficient. Even today many people don't think of Amazon as a dot-com company—they say, "I use it every day, it's wonderful, and it's such a gigantic company . . . it couldn't just leave, go dark, and vanish . . . of course it works. It survived the bubble, it made a profit. It has to work!" Millions of people who aren't interested in economics agree: it has to be able to survive because we all love it so much.

Friends, it would be a better world if that's how things worked, if a sense of moral certitude fortified our markets. That world is not our world, but even if it was, I don't think Amazon would deserve to be spared—there's a lot of history and debt to answer for. I remember the day we sent out a press release announcing the tremendous news that the next day we would be sending out another press release that would announce . . . something. I remember the stock spiking ten points, the fevered speculation by different media sources, and then the next day, when it turned out we'd just opened some new product categories (lead ingot shipping and secondhand meat), the stock dropped five points. I don't think the public noticed that we held on to five of those points, but we did. I remember seeing the PR staff in the cafeteria and smiling, knowing that they had scored a slam dunk.

For me, the realization that things might be very wrong started there. Not only might I not fit into Amazon's glorious future, but Amazon itself might share my confusion about what it was and where it was going. I was unwilling even to think about it because if we were wrong not just in our predictions but in our *spirit,* then we would be wrong in a way so grotesque that it would make me paranoid even to speak of it. Where's the line between irrational exuberance and fraud? I didn't want to find out.

I didn't know what my job was, but I was busy all the time, frightfully busy, just like everyone else. One thing I did know—I was responsible for going through the mail queue of unsolicited business proposals that got sent in to Amazon and picking out the gems.

Just so we understand each other: good business proposals do not come via unsolicited email. The odds that ShinyPanteez87@aol.com should be bought out and have a "Shiny Panties" tab on the homepage are somewhat remote. But since we wanted many of the people soliciting us to link to us, it took the hired hands of BizDev to take care of them. Thus, I and my colleagues would dutifully go into the slush piles and search for potential associates.

It was breathtaking to see the breadth and scope of bad unsolicited business plans that were emailed to Amazon.

If we were to talk about all the bad business plans that came through the channel, you'd be reading this chapter for a lunar month. And if we were only going to talk about the bad business plans that Amazon approved and bankrolled, you'd still be reading for a night and a day. So let's just pick one. One simple company. In fact, let's pick the one that was used as the shining example of what I should aspire to find. My group's vice president, who is still working at Amazon as of this writing, told me, "Michael, when you're going through these proposals, I want you to pick out only those businesses that have the same strong fundamentals, the same core values, as our new partner, Pets.com. Pets.com is the pinnacle and essence of what we're shooting for. Pets.com is exactly the kind of people we want to be in bed with."

So let's talk about Pets.com. Pets.com was the first mover in the pet space. *First mover* is a dot-com-era term derived from the popular board game Monopoly™. It made a great analogy for investors because everybody knew Monopoly™ and liked it. Nobody was interested in models that weren't sexy to investors, like the Land Mine™ model, in which e-commerce is a horrific battlefield where prices are a race to the bottom, there is no brand loyalty, and everyone loses limbs and lives after overextending and borrowing on margin.

Instead, you pretend that your business is a square on the Monopoly™ board. You showed up first on Park Place, you bought it, and now no one else can compete with you on the net because you own that space. You were first, so given the principle of time dilation no one will ever be able to catch up to you. In Monopoly™ you spend, beg, borrow, and steal as much as possible at the beginning of the game so that you'll be able to own property and thereby control the board in the endgame: it works every time in the game, and it would be the same with dot-coms. You can then build hotels and houses on the property and when other companies land on you, at some point in the future, you'll get all of their money. It sounds faintly ridiculous, but it was the leading Internet business model for a number of years.

Besides being the first mover, Pets.com also had a fantastic brand that was very recognizable, which was a big deal at the time: this was the era when someone was paid $7.5 million cash for the URL business.com. Keep in mind that Pets.com hadn't yet committed to spending $500 million on promoting a sock puppet, so their judgment wasn't entirely suspect.

In truth what really sold Amazon on Pets.com was an amazing PowerPoint presentation. PowerPoint was a holy tool to the dot-com world—it was the canvas on which your aspirations were painted. In this world of far-off results, the box and the ribbon were always more important than the item itself. PowerPoint was the universal language used to pitch these abstract ideas that could be turned into cash from the pockets of investors.

Even by the heady standards of the day, the Pets.com chart was really stunning. It was a piece of fine art that captured the eye and compelled attention, spreading like a mind virus through the entire company. Jeff used it, everyone used it once they saw it—it was as addictive to run as it was to watch.

It had a deceptively simple core. The presenter would put the PowerPoint graph up and then say, "This bar represents U.S. book sales last year." And as the first bar grew it would make this noise, *BoooMP!* Then he would say, "This bar represents sales in the pet market last year." And a second bar would grow beside the first, making a much louder *BOOOOOMMMPPP!!!* And then sometimes he'd show it

again: *BoooMP! BOOOOOMMMPPP!!!* That was all he had
to do, because throughout the room, everyone would be thinking the same profound thoughts in unison: *That one's bigger!
That one's bigger than the little one! It's like three times bigger!
Oh my God, we're going to be rich!*

Of course, the first problem was that the *BOOOOOM-
MMPPP!!!* bar represented *total* American pet sales in the previous year, but Pets.com did not actually sell live animals of
any kind—that cut down Pets.com's potential sales pretty sub-
stantially. Of the remaining sales, a huge percentage was made
up of dirt. You see, cats don't use your toilet and dogs don't eat
filet mignon. Dogs eat dog food, which looks like dirt and
tastes like dirt, and cats poop in cat litter, which *is* dirt. And
they both need a lot of this dirt to survive. In fact, 80 percent of
Pets.com's business was this dirt. Pets.com was in the gravel-
shipping business.

The Pets.com people spun this as a positive, and the spin
was so vigorous and counterintuitive that it could give you
whiplash. *This is great, this is actually great. It'll generate a lot
of churn to the website, they'll need to keep coming back and
back. Hold on, I'm seeing something . . . yeah . . . subscriptions! Yes! We'll set up a subscription service for cat litter or
dog food so they can have it automatically sent to them every
couple of weeks. They'll keep coming back to the website to
check in and that will boost our metrics numbers, which will
boost the stock and that's better than money. Further, they'll
grow to trust us from seeing us in their inbox, we'll develop a
relationship, and then we can cross-promote other goods and
services that they associate with the pet retail space like Cuisi-
narts and wall-to-wall carpeting. This is massive! This is all
upside, baby! Yeah!* [*Pumps arm; hoots.*]

The problem is that unlike corporations, most consumers are

not insane. After all, the consumer spends his life consuming, so he's really good at it. Imagine that you're this consumer, and you arrive at the checkout page of Pets.com to find totals that read:

$5 for your bag of cat litter
$45 for UPS ground shipping of said litter
=
$50 for a bag of dirt

You would then probably say, "Fuck you—no! No, I'm not gonna pay fifty dollars for you to ship me some fucking rocks in a bag. I'm going to get out of my La-Z-Boy and walk my lazy ass down the street to the store."

But Pets.com thought of this. *Yes, we understand there's going to be a lot of resistance on the sell-through in passing that price point on to the consumer, we know that, we accept that, that's clear. Okay. We are going to call this a "loss leader," we are going to absorb those losses, pay for the shipping, and make that a loss leader for us. We are going to lose money on this part of our business, we are going to lose money on this 80 percent of our business, we understand, we're clear. Everything's cool. Shhhh. Look at the puppet. Lalalalalala. Look over there at the shiny puppet. Lovely.*

Occasionally some brave employee would ask, gently and hesitantly, the most obvious question: "How, uh, how are we going to, how are we going to make . . . money? I'm just, I'm just, I'm just . . . asking." Everyone would stare at the poor bastard. "I'm just, you know . . . I mean—not for me. I don't want to know. I just mean, if people ask us, like the media, what . . . ah . . . what should we tell them?"

Don't worry your pretty little head. We're going to make it up on the high-margin items.

Oh yes. Of course. The high-margin items, the salvation of

every e-commerce venture. I don't know how many times I've been lounging around my mansion with my thirty Persian cats when suddenly I've thought, *You know, I should get all my cats jeweled platinum cat collars with inlaid diamonelles, and then on top of that I think I'll order thirty—no, sixty!—custom velour scratching posts so I can mount a bunch of them onto the walls and some on the floor so they can just* play. *And I will do all of this through Pets.com, because they did such a great job with my four thousand pounds of cat litter* .

No. This doesn't happen. Only crazy people buy this much high-end pet paraphernalia, and crazy people are not early adopters of new technologies like the Internet. There are some barriers to entry:

1. They're crazy.
2. They have no money.
3. They live in asylums.
4. They don't have computers.

But I don't even know if I'm qualified to be speaking, because I was there, I saw the *BoooMP!* and *BOOOOOM-MMMPPP!!!* and I told everyone I knew, "Dude! It's bigger! It's bigger!" I went on and on to my future in-laws about the infallible nature of technology investing, and I would have staked my children's trust funds on the certain demand there would be for electronic dog gravel delivery in 2010.

➤ So let's do the math. I'm in a department. I cannot really tell you what it is we actually do, or even what we think we do. I have some defined duties, but in any case I am only answerable to a manager who will no longer speak to me and therefore cannot assign me any further duties.

I have never been in a more perfect work environment.

It was as though I'd been allowed into the graduate school I had always dreamed of. That's how I looked at it, and I was diligent about pursuing this opportunity: I signed up for every tech-industry email list I could find. I got subscriptions to the *Industry Standard, Fast Company, Silicon Alley Reporter, Business 2.0,* and other periodicals with even more effective-sounding names like *WORK!* and *VICTORY!* I read them all day long until I could walk the walk and jive the low-hanging fruit, the first-mover advantage, and the vertical scaling.

It was social hacking. I could hack this company and get it to give up the goods for me, more rewards than I'd ever imagined I would have in my lifetime. I'd bleach my hair really blond, lose weight, learn to snowboard, make new friends. I would be a goddamned net executive.

14

Exit Interview

As defining dates go, it's hard to do better than December 31, 1999. Between the obvious fin de siècle talk and the charmingly apocalyptic Y2K predictions, it garnered a lot of street cred in advance. Everyone I knew was preparing for the intense letdown you feel every New Year's Eve at about one A.M. when you realize you got dressed up for *this*. The feeling is usually strongest just as you are holding your date's hair out of the toilet in which she is getting sick.

Millennial New Year's took this to the next level. Except for Walt Disney, no one would be seeing the next one, which gave many people permission to engage in a race to the height of excess—no amount of money was too much to spend. Rich technophiles flew party jets from time zone to time zone, fleeing the terminator across the globe. Others had lush parties on mountaintops, drank champagne cooled by Arctic seawater, or waited in bunkers for the Internet to come crashing down as it flipped from 99 to 00. "Stupid money" flew from person to person as in a game of marbles. It was a coming-out party for the tech revolution.

My generation, the hyperrelaxed slackers who became hyperactive dot-commers, had been looking forward to the twenty-first century our entire lives. It was our birthright—we hoped that everything that had come before was to be prelude and overture to a *real* digital revolution that would change the world so completely that the boomers would finally give us the keys to the city. You could read about it in *Wired*. In the dot-com world the twenty-first century had always been envisioned as an era of unrelenting triumph, like Leni Riefenstahl on crystal meth, and no celebration could be too large to celebrate the fact that the future had finally arrived.

I was in San Francisco with Jean-Michele. I had made a small stab at millennial decadence myself by impulsively buying tickets for the weekend just twenty-four hours earlier. They'd been cheap because of lurking fears that all the planes would drop out of the air sometime around the switchover. I had then scored a cute faux French-style hotel room. I felt like a swashbuckling romantic—I hadn't told Jean-Michele about any of it.

On the last day of the twentieth century I woke her up at six A.M. Unfortunately, she was a mess from the night before—we had been drinking until four, so when I woke her up with the news that we had to pack a bag, right now, immediately, in her still-drunk half-sleep she thought the Cossacks were coming to kill us—a fear instilled early by Babcia—which resulted in her freaking out in the bathroom for a while. But once I convinced her we were not going to be slaughtered by the Horde she got into it.

We didn't have a plan for the evening itself—Jane of the Shredded Cheese had given us directions to a giant party hosted by some character named Chicken John who would do *craaazy* things with public nudity and hip late-nineties weirdness (principally more nudity, glitter, and ecstasy), but that sounded exhausting. We also almost ate a special prix fixe French dinner for four hundred dollars each, but cooler heads prevailed and we admitted we weren't really ever hungry enough to eat four hundred dollars worth of dinner.

We ended up wandering around San Francisco, a city I had never been to, drinking in the streets. At midnight the fireworks went up just as they did everywhere. We were riding in a taxi as it happened, and we kissed and listened to the people shouting and crying out in celebration at each and every intersection we passed, waves of drunk happiness crashing over our cab.

A few hours later we were back in our hotel, too wired to sleep, watching MSNBC, and like the rest of the planet, passing judgment on the festivities of other cities.

"Paris wins." I was pretty certain.

"Yep, seems to be the consensus. Look at that." On our small screen the Eiffel Tower was bursting into flames as it transfigured into light.

"Damn. It's sad about the English."

"Yeah, the giant Ferris wheel is weak."

"I kept hoping it would break free and roll into the Thames. It's so big . . . that would rock," I said. Jean-Michele looked unimpressed.

"You always want some big explosion. Poor England. They

try so hard and then, wham, there are the French with all their class and taste."

"Stupid French."

"What do you have against the French?"

"Well—" I stopped. "You know, I've been bashing them for so long I don't even know anymore."

"Figures." The TV had switched to West Coast news and everyone was taking potshots at the France of the West Coast, Seattle. "What a shame about them canceling the New Year's events—I'm glad we got out of town and did this."

"Hard to believe they'd cancel New Year's because of some 'terrorist threat.'"

"They thought that guy they caught was planning to blow up the Space Needle."

"Yeah, I heard that. Terrorists attack America. I think I saw that cable movie." I yawned. "I am glad that it's been peaceful everywhere and nobody's computer exploded."

"Yeah, it did go smoothly. The mayor certainly looks stupid now."

"Yeah. He'll be punished for making Seattle look chicken." I turned off the sound on the TV where a talking head was analyzing the lack of news. "It's so quiet here. I don't know what I expected . . . you know, I think deep down I thought something was going to happen."

"Like Y2K?" She smiled.

"Not that, but . . . something. Is that insensitive?"

"A little. You're always looking for drama."

It got later, we made love, and she fell asleep beside me, but I was sleepless. When I'm overwrought I often find myself imagining how immense the universe is and how many different forces are at work: our earth spinning on its axis at thousands of miles an hour, that spinning top tracking around the sun even faster, this sun receding from its local group of stars in this arm of our galaxy, which is rotating at its own impossible rate, and so on, forever. If you add up just the vectors we can track, we'd already be moving at half the speed of light. Relativity vertigo.

I held on to the edge of the bed, willing myself to stay in place. I could feel the earth beneath me and my own place on it, a speck holding on by gravity and luck at these terrible speeds. If gravity failed there'd be no warning—just a sudden rushing and we'd be hurled off this dirty globe by the earth's spin, sprung free into space in one instant. I could not shake the certain feeling that everything was ending.

Warren and I had stayed in sporadic contact—we were both busy in different worlds so there wasn't much chance to see each other. Right after San Francisco I got an email from him.

```
To:mdaisey@amazon.com
From:warren@amazon.com
Subject:looking for info

M~

Writing you from down here in the belly of the beast.
Could you check on something? Word around the camp-
fire here is that corporate has cut all ibuprofen as
a cost-saving measure. No one here can believe that.
Let me know if you know the shot, and if you still
have painkiller. If so, interoffice us some because
we need it.

~W
```

I checked our office supply cabinet: you could still get high with dry erase markers, but there was no aspirin, Tylenol, nothing. I asked around and at first nobody seemed to know anything. Then, slowly, word spread that this was indeed a cost-cutting measure recently implemented.

To:warren@amazon.com
From:mdaisey@amazon.com
Subject:Re:looking for info

You're right--I can't believe it, they have cut off the painkillers. Christ, I can't believe that we'd save *that* much money--I mean, will that be in the investor report?: "Amazon achieved profitability in the 4th quarter by removing aspirin and water fountains and requiring employees to bring their own toilet paper." This stinks.

md

Almost immediately from Warren:

To:mdaisey@amazon.com
From:warren@amazon.com
Subject:warning

M~

Daisey, this is a very bad sign. You can brand me alarmist, but when they start cutting perks in a company that DOES NOT GIVE YOU A DESK we need to be on

```
alert. I've heard that there might be layoffs in Jan-
uary. Keep your head low and your gun handy.
```

```
~W
```

I had to read the last message twice before I believed it. Lay-offs? At Amazon? How could a company based on constant growth justify needing *fewer* people? Selective firings for incompetence, yes, but there could never be layoffs . . . we were Amazon.com, the fastest growing company in the history of the world.

At the same time it was hard to ignore the aspirin situation. I couldn't forget what my friend Alex had said about leaving Microsoft. He had started there early, made his fortune, and exited. I asked him why he'd left and he said: "Pens." Microsoft, with its monopoly sustained by lying and shivving the competition, suddenly started stocking only Bics instead of nice Sharpies and rollertips. When that started happening Alex took it as a sign that things had finally started going south. He told me, "What's the point of working for Stalin if you aren't even going to get a fur coat?" I nodded sagely and privately thought it was stupid . . . but here I was, and the aspirin was gone.

The news was delivered on a Tuesday morning in a confer-ence room, as it would be at so many other dot-coms. BizDev managers and vice presidents hemmed and hawed and stum-bled through the excuses, for which we were forgiving, since no one there had any experience in delivering bad news. When we left the conference room our fate was clear: reorganized. Our subset of BizDev would be pared off from the main body and "reorged" as its own group. No one was being let go, but we would no longer be in BizDev, close to the movers and shakers. We were being sent to be a special operations group in customer service.

You could have heard a pin drop when they told us. Most of us in my immediate group had fought our way up from CS, so it was amazing to see the brightly scrubbed faces of the BizDev folks explaining how this was a blessing, how we'd grow more fully and have promotional opportunities within customer service. Our group knew the score, and it was clear that we'd prefer a firing squad to being thrown back into the gerbil cage.

Now BizDev would be free to be an enclave of right-thinking MBAs who would transform Amazon into a normal company, a company that would post profits and thrive in the long term. Hyperdarwinism had caught up with us, and in that room we listened as our friendly, affable former colleagues explained why without opposable thumbs we really weren't going to be that useful to the cause anymore. Come back when you've received your Stanford MBA in the mail. Gotcha. Catch ya later.

➤ Just a few days after Black Tuesday I went to the bathroom and sat down upon the toilet, as I am wont to do. A piece of paper was sticking out of the sanitary-toilet-cover-dispensing thing. Remarkably, the paper spoke to me. It said, in a high and reedy voice, "Michael . . . read me . . . and I will ruin your life."

"Paper, what do you want with me? I am on the toilet."

"Read me . . . read me and see."

"This better be worth it."

"Read me."

I was intrigued, so I took the paper and read it.

I'll never know who left the piece of paper there, and I will always wonder: did someone hate his colleagues? Was it an amateur anarchist? Or perhaps a disaffected temp—that's what I had been once, and the act captured something of my own style. I will never know the answer, but the result of his efforts was clear.

Someone had printed out an Excel spreadsheet from human resources that listed the crown jewels: the salaries, stock options, and strike prices of every single person in my department. In the charged atmosphere of BizDev, these numbers were nuclear launch codes.

"Now your life is ruined," said the paper. "Bwahahahahha."

And, oddly enough, it was. I sat, reading down the list of outlandish figures that were so much larger than I had even dreamed or imagined. I felt a strange detachment from the hot and cold fury that bubbled in me—some of these people were halfwits and were making more money than I could imagine spending without breaking laws. I had always known this inequality existed and that it was vast, but there's a gap between knowing about it and having it smack you in the face suddenly.

I wasn't certain how to react. I knew I should wipe, get up, wash my hands both literally and figuratively, and get on with my life. I did not do this. Instead, I took the paper to the photocopier and made many copies of it, obsessively, the same way I would copy my hand again and again while watching the light spill out of the green glass edges.

I then took it to the other people in my group who I now knew were, like me, at the pecuniary bottom of the list. I gave them their papers and with each of them it was as though I had casually handed over the Golden Apple: "Oh, what's thi—

Ahhhhhhhhhh! I've gone blind! Why, why did you make me read this? You bastard!"

I told them the truth: "I don't know why I did this. I thought it would make me feel better." But it didn't make me feel better. Not yet.

 # We had fallen on hard times.

Between the demotion to customer service and my terrible bathroom revelations, everyone in my group had lost all ambition and order. No one worked. It wasn't a planned strike of any kind—we had just halted in a confusion that deepened into melancholy and despair. One day stretched into two, then three . . . soon it had been a week, and now we were having a meeting because it was becoming clear that a very passive-aggressive, low-key, Seattle-style mutiny was going on. Employee #5 called us together—I heard about it secondhand because we still weren't talking.

It felt like there was a storm system in the room, and in the tradition of great men everywhere, Employee #5 shocked everyone by rising to the occasion. Granted, he still could not make eye contact, but while staring down at the table he told us how things would be. He told us how he had hoped to keep us in BizDev, how he had no control over the situation, how it was all right to be angry. He spoke simply and clearly about the company, which sounded strange to my ears, and I realized only later that what I might have been hearing was frankness without propaganda.

He was a smart guy who had lucked into a great place, and he loved the company—he loved the idea of selling books on the net. It was cool. He'd configured the first databases and worked day and night to make the website work for those first tens and hundreds of customers. He'd never signed on to sell farm equipment and auction stereo systems and track customer data down to the micron, but he'd made $300 million so he could never complain. Still, you could hear in his voice his regret, how he missed the ownership of the competent, resourceful geek: to know your systems backward and forward, to be able to tell by how long a terminal takes to respond whether the build is lagging. Little things. I felt ashamed that I had never realized that there might be larger reasons why Employee #5 wished he were a vice president. His baby had grown and grown and been taken away from him.

He told us all, "The company you worked for, the company you joined, is dead. No one else will tell you this. It is dead already. This is a new company, and there are new rules and we can't go back. It's the way things are and it isn't going to change, and if this isn't the place you fell in love with, you should bite your tongue or you should walk. We all know that at Amazon you can't make it half-committed. That won't change." He looked very tired, and I knew he was speaking to himself, but I heard him clearly.

➤ I found myself snapping at Jean-Michele, nervous and skittish. Meanwhile I was constantly going over the list I'd found, as though it would give me some answers, calculating the current and future worths of my colleagues: $6 million, $8 million, $10 million, $9 million—*damn, that's why he has that BMW! Jesus, what a fool I've been!*

I was so furious, more furious than I had ever been. Simultaneously, I was ashamed of my fury because of what it revealed about me. This was greed, but I wanted to spin it and make it be about entitlement, so I could feel that I deserved $5 million. But even I couldn't swallow that self-deception. I'd never wanted money, never in my life. I wanted to write and perform and tell stories—I'd never thought of myself as the kind of person who craves material things.

But at the same time, I couldn't account for this fury that would not relent, and it continued to grow until I broke through to a new level of furious that I had never reached before. I began wondering, *Why am I so angry? When did I become entitled to this? What changed? When did that happen? Exactly when? What day was it?* And the strangest thing was that I knew—I actually remembered standing in the shower with the water pouring down on me, the inconstant pressure pulsing up and down while I was doing the math, playing a game called If. If the stock kept going up just 20 percent a year . . . If I could stay onboard for three more years . . . If I could just get another option grant at just 20 percent more every single year—which wasn't much in those days—I was going to be worth . . . $3 million. In four years. Me.

In that moment the equation became part of me, was taken up by my mind and planted deep within my heart like a seed, growing within and through me, from a seed into a plant then into a tree of certainty to which I nailed a sign that said: WAIT. WAIT. WAIT. Don't be rash. Don't leave. You don't know what you're doing with your time, you don't know what it is that you are spending yourself on—think of the future. Be sensible. It's like communism, but then you get paid: put everything of yourself into this machine for five years and at the end you'll be rewarded for your devotion and you can take up your life where you left off.

The problem is it doesn't work. And it's not because the stock eventually tanks or the economy rolls down into the mud. It's because of what my mother used to tell me: "Work is love made visible," to which I thought, *That's some Puritan horse-shit.* But I found myself hearing her words as I sat up at night. I was afraid that like so many things in this life, she might be right. I was afraid that this would mean that what you do with your time, day in and day out, is what you would be judged by and what counted. Not the plays I never finished and the writing I was too busy to write down, not the comedy on the side. My identity would be my job, and when I was asked who I was the answer would be "aspiring midlevel manager."

And titles aside, pride aside, what was I actually *doing*? Nothing. I was hoping to learn snowboarding and waiting for someone to hand me a winning lottery ticket. How was that better than performing in an unheated garage? I had been a directionless artist and now I was a directionless office drone. Some have said that the dot-com era failed because the riches attracted greedy folks—parasites. I was afraid to think too deeply about whether I fell into that category.

I have always been a very clever person. This is a serious flaw in my character, and only now did I see clearly where I had led myself. When I arrived in BizDev I had been so proud of myself for being so clever, for having walked in off the street and tricked everyone and carved out my own place. It was only now that I could see that they had never cared whether that report was real or not—it had never entered their minds to check. Why would they have checked? No one can check facts in the New Economy. Instead they examined the words I had chosen, the fine paper I had used to print out the report, the binder's fake leather texture, and the sharp laser printing in suave 13-point Lucida Grande. They looked all this over and thought, *This guy knows how to spin, how to twist things into shape. This guy can do very well here.* And the worst part was that they were right.

And then I thought: *Fuck. I've gone too far now. I've*

thought my way down too many of these roads. And I'm not going to be able to forget that I thought these things—I know them. So even though I still love the company, and even though I have nowhere to go, I'm going to have to quit.

➤ Cody helped me clean out my desk. I needed help carrying everything because I couldn't resist taking every last stapler, Sharpie, and Post-it I could swipe from the supply closets. I couldn't tell if it was a case of old habits dying hard or a premonition that I wouldn't be returning to the office world anytime soon.

Like the desks of cubedwellers everywhere, mine had become a dustbin of forgotten and arcane swag—free stuff other companies gave out to make you love them. I shoveled leftover CueCATs into moving boxes along with six or seven different Amazon baseball caps, mousepads, and keychains. It's a little sad to see logo-branded junk having more longevity than a career.

"You don't need to leave," Cody said as he helped pack another box of Kozmo.com penlights. "The reorg actually made it more likely that you'll have a career path, and with some clout in CS you'll never have to deal with metrics again. Then do your time and collect the options. You won't even be under Employee #5. It's easy."

"I know." I put a ream of copier paper into a box. "You're right. Pragmatically speaking, things have never been better for me here."

"So?"

I taped another box shut. "I don't want a job that makes sense. I'm done here. Hand me another box." He did. "I know this isn't practical," I said.

Then he came out with it. "A lot of people around here are tempted to do the same. The layoffs have started, and with all the reorging . . . I don't know."

"Everyone's waking up every day scared?"

"Fucking terrified." He smiled grimly and put the last of my boxes on the dolly. "What's your plan?"

"Load these boxes in the car, go home, take a nap."

"I mean your long-range plan."

"That is my long-range plan."

▶ It was an orderly exit. I gave my two weeks, collected vacation time, watched my email and terminal go dark, had lunch at a generic Pan-Asian hotel restaurant with my colleagues, knowing I would never see them again. Employee #5 bought lunch but he never said goodbye. Human resources failed to show up for my exit interview, which was great because the only exit interview I want in this life is the one at the end with God.

I left the building with my Amazon ID burning in my pocket, a cancelled Golden Ticket.

To: jeff@amazon.com
From: mdaisey@amazon.com
Subject: au revoir

It's hard to believe that this is goodbye, Jeff. After all the trials we've both been through, it seems like no amount of words could express the feelings I'm sure you have. I know it's hard to see now, but I have faith that you'll be able to go on without me. You have to.

Don't forget all the great times we had, Jeff, like when we drank that leftover beer and you pissed all over Joe Galli's desk. You said you were "marking territory"...oh, how we laughed. Good times, Jeff.

You must be afraid, facing the coming days without me by your side. That's understandable, and you're going to make some mistakes, but you've always had a knack for making brilliant discoveries in the midst of total disaster--and I think you'll need that in spades. You're the Man of the Year now, and that's a tall height to fall from...Don't forget all the things we've talked about--low-hanging fruit, the first-mover advantage, the sweet spot in a great tennis racket. You're a great talker.

I still think you should have listened to me and dumped Auctions, but you're on your own now--it's all up to you. You're an exceptional man, and I know you'll keep hustling for as long and as far as you can. I look forward to reading about your exploits over the coming years, and I expect you to keep me entertained, Jeff.

As for me, I'm hanging up my idealism for now. I'd tell you what I was doing next, how I was going to leverage my time at Amazon.com into a brilliant future, but the truth is you wouldn't hear me. I'm falling out of Amazon Time, and the distance between us will swell until you are a million years ahead of me, forging the future. I tried to keep up, but I'm never going to be the man you need me to be. Nothing I will do after Amazon will ever be inter-esting to you.

Be careful, Jeff. People can be cruel, and I fear for you in the coming years--I feel ashamed to leave you now, in the hour when you will need me the most. I hope you'll forgive me.

md

P.S. I wanted to thank you for letting me keep my badge. I'm not certain what it's good for, but I intend to find out.

Subject: au revoir

15

Museum of Ham

As though trying to set a land-speed record for regret, I actually became unhappy with my decision before I had even left the building. The stock was still trading near a hundred, close to its all-time high, and I had just taken a huge equity investment in that position, set it on fire, kicked it out to the curb, and pissed on it before watching the garbage men take it away. What had I been thinking? What gesture of self-discovery was I making? I had no job. I had no prospects. My previous work history included a B.A. in an obscure branch of philosophy that made people snicker and a rich tapestry of menial temping positions. I had just turned my back on the only grown-up place I had ever worked, and there was no end to the friends and family calling me every day to tell me what a total and complete idiot I was:

"You did what? Amazon was the only good thing that ever happened to you!"

"You would have been rich in a year, maybe two. Fucking hippie-ass moron."

"Hope you're not still planning on marrying that nice girl."

"Oh my God . . . you've ruined your life."

(That last one was my mother.)

So it came to pass that I was unplugged from the great clock of Amazon Time, and discovered that when you left you suffered the painful dislocation of its obverse, Unemployed Time.

And lo, the daytime TV did flow like honeyed wine! And lo, did I become acquainted with Judge Judy, and Judge Joe Brown, and all the judges of daytime who sat in attendance on my court and watched me spend my days and nights curled in a fetal position with the remote.

I was captivated by *Who's the Boss?*, where Alyssa Milano was perpetually sprouting into naughty adolescence and Tony Danza proved endlessly that he had only one character, one voice, and one dimension, but was still strangely endearing. I studied *The Price Is Right*, where I learned not how much a can of lima beans cost in real life but how much it cost in Game Show World. I analyzed the two Darrins of *Bewitched*, contrasting their behavior to determine which one might have wife-beating tendencies based on his Rage Index in *Cosmo*—it was a dead heat.

And the advertisements! People who have never professionally vegetated in front of their daytime and late-night noncable television have no idea how insidious they are. From watching those compilation album ads I fell in love with songs, but only the six seconds of each one I heard on the ad. I would sing the one lyric I knew in the shower over and over:

This old wheel,
Is going to come around once more
This old wheel,
Is going to come around once more
This old wheel,
Is going to come around once more

Endless fun! With time I became susceptible to suggestions. I had a newfound conviction that air conditioner repair was a valid career choice. I started talking about it as a self-mocking put-down, but as the ad kept being replayed and I became more depressed I started to believe in it.

"Jean-Michele, many people are getting their degrees every day."

"Shut the fuck up."

"Why are you trying to crush my dreams?"

"I am not crushing your dreams, because you do not dream of being an air conditioner repairman."

"Think of our children—little Benito, so proud of his daddy cleaning and refurbishing air conditioners."

"First, we have no children."

"Benito!"

"Shut up. Second, the fact that you're using a Mexican name for our child is borderline racist and implies that you don't take seriously the idea of this manual labor job."

"We named him Benito after Mussolini—Benito is Italian!"

"Why the fuck are we naming our imaginary son after Mussolini?"

"How can you accuse me of borderline racism?"

"If you're not racist, take the trash out!"

"What?"

"If you can do manual labor, manually labor the trash out to the Dumpster."

"This is a transparent ploy to get your trash taken out!"

"I'd just like to enjoy the sight of you doing something."

"Fuck you."

"That would be a change of pace as well."

I stormed out, taking the trash with me. I didn't separate the plastic recycling or the glass bottles, which passes for protest when you're unemployed.

I also discovered that I had become net addicted. Before Amazon I had not actually gone online very often, but after websurfing pretty regularly for thirty-five hours a week I discovered that without T1 speeds I got the shakes. Trying to satisfy myself with dial-up was like sucking a bowling ball through a straw. The weird part was that I couldn't say what it was I was doing with all that time and bandwidth—I was not much more informed, considering how many news sites I had bookmarked, nor was I particularly more effective at gathering information. I had begun using the net as a virtual bookshelf on which I could put a lot of my thoughts, and as a consequence, when it went away it took a significant piece of my brain with it. This was unfortunate, as I needed my brain to help me set the VCR to tape *Buffy* while I was doing my air conditioner repair coursework.

I had many lesser loves, but my chief obsession in this time of strife was Jerry. His show came on at eleven A.M. and I would sit ritualistically with my enormous bowl of cereal, hungry for knowledge. To say that I got very *into* the stories would be a massive understatement. I would call Jean-Michele at her real job and tell her what I was seeing.

"There is a couple on right now and they're fighting . . . hold on . . . her name is Wilamina, and I'm really concerned, because Rick is married to her but has been sleeping with her half-sister, Janey. Okay, Janey is coming out . . . and Wilamina and she are fighting . . . okay, they're being separated. They're swearing. Jesus, they're sisters—they should turn around and kick this scrawny man's ass for playin' them like this. They just can't communicate, that's the real crisis. Okay, Janey has taken off her shirt to show the crowd why Rick's going to keep sleeping with her. That's an odd choice."

"Michael, listen to me."

"Okay."

"Do not call me again unless you have been killed."

"Okay." Click.

I also took phone calls all day long as I lay inert on the floor. After all, I had left Amazon.com's business development department at the very height of the New Economy—things were still red-hot. I didn't even need to put my résumé out there because the drums sounded all the way through the jungle: "FIVE MILES EAST . . . SOMEONE AVAILABLE . . . FROM AMAZON . . . STRIKE FAST." And heeding the call, the headhunters came.

They called me day after day. It was awful, wonderful, and decadent—they were offering me new jobs at big companies with big important salaries, the kind of really foolish money some of my colleagues had been making. It was apparently not clear that I knew *nothing*, that I had no qualifications whatsoever except my former job title. All I could do was breathe, send and receive email, and tell stories.

I told some of them this, or at least hinted at it, and was told that it didn't matter—I had been at Amazon.com, the Mecca of the dot-com world, and in business development no less. That meant I was freshly minted gold, and no amount of incompetence could rub off the reputation I hadn't earned. Buy.com, eToys, Toys "R" Us, recruiting firms, contract project-management groups—they stood in line and made their offers based on ether and the pleasant sound of my voice.

I was stuck. I had left a job I liked and a company I loved because I had these fuzzy principles and I needed to purify myself and change the way I lived. At the same time, I had no money, no prospects, and no plan . . . nor could I actually explain what I thought I was doing, even to myself. I was afraid not to take one of these good jobs I didn't want because I was terrified that if I didn't act they would vanish and I would never be employable again. I didn't want to say yes and I was afraid to say no, so I untied this Gordian knot in the most craven way—I said yes to *everybody.*

It was as though I had become some kind of fucked-up debutante, taking each and every phone call, flirting with every job offer, and keeping them all dangling on the line, day after day. I was noncommittal because I wanted to avoid direct offers, but the more I played hard to get, the more my value increased in their eyes. I had strings of start dates at places from Ohio to Atlanta all through the summer. It was disgusting, impossible, and very typical—it might have gone on for a really long time if it weren't for the giant enormous baby.

You may be familiar with this episode of *Jerry.* At the top of the show, Jerry stepped toward the camera and said, "Ladies and gentlemen, I'd like to present this giant enormous baby." And this guy comes out. He's thirty-five or forty years old, he has lank, greasy hair, and the fat is just rolling off his body, which is completely naked except for a little cloth diaper he's wearing. As it registers that it is a *diaper,* for Christ's sake, he begins to waddle forward in a grotesque, adult parody of a child's movements. He wants his rattle. I feel this pressure in my chest and my hand rises to my mouth like in those old-school horror movies because I see him, I recognize him, and all I can say is, "That's me . . . that's me . . . I am the Giant Enormous Baby."

And then I was really depressed—depressed in a way that made all that had preceded it seem like a blissful warm-up. It was Black Dog time. I lay unmoving before the television. Food wrappers and trash orbited around me, attracted by the immobile gravitational fields of my inert flesh. Jean-Michele would get up in the morning and go off to work, telling me gently, "I'm going to work now. Do you need anything?"

"I'm the Giant Enormous Baby."

"I know, honey, I know." She smiled at me, trying to show me how people cope. "Just try to get up and leave the house today, just try to take a walk around the block. Do you want me to turn on the TV?"

"No. I'm the Giant Enormous Baby, goddamn it."

"I'm aware of that."

"Please kill me."

"Shhhhh." She left.

➤ Clinicians say that geographic cures don't work, but sometimes they are your only option. The only resource I had was a lump of cash money from selling my stock. When I left I had sold what stock I had vested, which was nowhere near the full amount.

Just as an aside, if for some reason you are receiving your compensation from your employer in stock, please be careful. Stock options are taxed hugely; they make you think you are some sort of fat-cat billionaire when in reality you are leaving with a box of leftover lasagna and a season of *Laugh In* on Betamax. I sold my Amazon stock near the all-time high, at

$96, and I joined the company relatively early, yet when you add my stock sale cash to my salary, subtract taxes, and divide that number by the hours I worked, I ended up making about $6.85 an hour. I would have gotten a better deal at Taco Bell.

It was an uncomfortably middling sum of money—too small to live on while lying on the floor for any length of time, but too large to fritter away on junk food and movie rentals. I was very uncomfortable with the entire proposition of having money, since I'd never had any before, not all in one piece, and it was freaking me out that I could have all this money and still be a baby. I thought what I needed to do was bury the money, maybe in the park, and then make a treasure map to it. Barring that, I was in favor of T-bills or some other investment that would be safer than Amazon stock, which is to say anything.

Jean-Michele thought I ought to spend all this money right then and get rid of it, just get it out of there, and then I wouldn't have to worry about it anymore and that would be a big relief for both of us. I was surprised by her zeal.

"You're always trying to get us to save and be sensible."

"That was before."

"Before what?"

"Before my fiancé lost his mind. Now I just want the money gone and you back—turn the sound on." An expert with the remote, I complied. It was a British Airways ad. Some London tarts were cackling about great overnight service. Jean-Michele immediately picked up the phone.

"What are you doing?"

"Spending the Devil's money. We're going on a trip."

"We are? Where?"

"We'll pick from what's available right now. Not San Francisco. Further."

"How far?"

She smiled. "Far enough to outrun all of this."

"Jesus. How far is that? What about your job? Are we talk-ing crazy, like, ah . . . Spain?"

Her eyes narrowed. "Yes. In fact, that will do nicely."

➤ It was the best thing she could have done for us. It was in Spain that Internet Time started to loosen its grip on me, because Spain is home to the Laziest People On Earth, and I love them so much! I love each and every lazy one of them. They drink lazy, they make love lazy, everything they do is lazy lazy lazy! It was wonderful, a perfect balm after my addiction to dot-com speed. I was entranced by the languorous way they refused to do simple tasks for one another.

"Manuel, bring me the wine."

"I cannot, Isabella, it is too far away."

"No, Manuel, it is not far from you. It is right there."

"I cannot."

"Reach out your arm."

"No, I am too tired. Let us sleep." And they slept.

Oh, I loved them! I would buy churros from a vendor on the street, and in the middle of the sale—Oh! we're both tired, let's take a little nap—we'd sleep. When we woke up we'd finish the transaction and he'd hand me my treat with a smile and a wave. It was magical!

Jean-Michele had been to Madrid before. When we landed she immediately took me by the arm.

"There's somewhere we have to go. It's the reason I wanted to come here."

"Where?"

"The Museum of Ham."

"We just spent our dot-com fortune to go to a ham museum?"

The Museo de Jamón, as it turns out, is a fabulously popular chain of pork-oriented sandwich stores throughout Spain. Jean-Michele was right—their *jamón y queso* sandwiches took ham and cheese to a whole new level I had never considered before, knocking me down and picking me back up again by my taste buds. They are well worth a small fortune, and I speak from experience.

Every day we wandered the streets. We never went to the Prado or did anything cultural, which was such a relief after endless years of microivy college-induced "learn about native cultures" brainwashing. I had never been in a place so beautiful that I was content to just soak my eyes in it rather than read endlessly about which king had died to build what roadway. Instead I sat in the marvelous sun-dappled plazas and drank. Drank beer, then wine, then beer, and then it was time for dancing, and then we would sleep. The clubs were open until dawn and we danced until four A.M., and then we'd go to cafes that were still open and bustling, everyone laughing and crying at the same time.

One night, just before dawn, we were eating olives and holding hands as a soprano from the opera sang, drunk and magnificent, for her dinner. The other singers pounded the table and shouted as she sang higher and higher. Her voice fluttered and rose again and again, dashing against the smoky rafters, and the longer she sang the more free food and wine was brought to their overflowing table by a laughing owner who directed the trays with the simplest finger motion indicating, "Give."

As we cheered her performance something broke inside of me, broke open, and I knew that I had been dead for a long time without realizing it. It was there, while I was completely drunk, that I finally started to dry out from my experiences at Amazon, the way lakebeds are only visible when the water has been drained. I could now see the bottom, and I was shocked by what I discovered—the things I had done, the ways I had thought, and the things I had failed to do.

I had missed the WTO riots, a signature event in Seattle's history. I not only hadn't rioted, I hadn't even gone down and gawked at the spectacle. Even worse, I remember standing around at work, talking with a gaggle of BizDev types, Republicans who didn't know it yet, about how it was unfortunate that these people were disrupting *commerce.* I actually used the word *commerce.* Commerce! I remember thinking that fall that if the Republicans got the White House it would probably result in a reduction in the capital gains tax, and that would be really good for me and my stock options . . . I mean, I would never vote for a Republican . . . would I? I couldn't tell.

I couldn't believe what I had become, how much I had changed, but it's an old story—one of the oldest. It's the delusion of immortality. When you're young, you think that you'll live forever. *Hey, check me out, I'm sixteen and I'm bulletproof.* This misconception generally fades around twenty-three, when you wake up in a Dumpster naked, covered in garbage, and you realize: *Oh, I'm not immortal; Jaegermeister is my kryptonite.*

Everyone knows that. What I didn't realize is there's a more seductive immortality: the immortality of the mind. You go through a lot in this life to figure out *who* you are, and the delusion is that now that you know, it is *fixed.* You paid to understand yourself, so now you do. You are constant and eternal and your nature isn't going to change—not without you knowing, anyway. Not because of a job. Not because of something you do for money.

That's not true. The truth is we're changing all the time,

each and every moment of every day, and there's nothing we can do about it. You never know the name of anything that can destroy you until it has passed. Only later, if you are lucky, can you say: *Oh, I'm still not immortal. This, too, was kryptonite.* Then you live with it and grow weaker, or you hide from it, or you put your hands inside of it and mold it, shape it into something small and heavy you can remember to carry in your pocket every day.

In a plaza in Madrid it is morning and the sun is already hot in the sky, casting long sharp shadows through the square. My future wife and I are sitting across from each other. Each of us has in front of us two glasses: beer and coffee—a poor man's speedball. The sun is beating down on us, and Jean-Michele speaks.

"You've changed. Just in the time we've been here, you've changed."

I stare up at the windows around the plaza. "I feel better. I feel . . . more."

She says quietly, "I missed you. I didn't realize that I missed you, but . . . I missed you."

"I guess I missed me too."

"When we go back home, all those job offers are still going to be there, all the recruiters. What are you going to do?" She's watching me, and I speak carefully.

"You know . . . there is something I could do that would make certain that no one would ever hire me again."

And God bless her, she doesn't say a word to stop me. She just lifts the third beer of the morning to her lips and says, "Good."

To: jeff@amazon.com
From: mdaisey@mac.com
Subject: laugh with me

I always wanted to make you laugh. Do you remember
this one?

Albania's economy collapsed in '97 because everybody in the country, 90% of them, entered the same
pyramid scheme. Everyone laughed and laughed at the
stupid Albanians, stupid because they entered a
club where they put in all their money, couldn't get
out, and needed to find five more suckers to join if
they wanted to keep their shirts. The kicker is,
when they asked the Albanians where they thought
the money was going to come from, they all said, "We
didn't know...we thought it was capitalism." Man, I
could laugh myself sick.

Did you hear that somebody broke back into Amazon
after getting laid off? He stood up on top of a
table in the cafeteria and laughed for five minutes.
He laughed like you--a brittle, joyous yelping in
panic-driven waves. When he finished he walked out.
No one touched him--they didn't want to catch the
disease of being laid off.

I always dreamed that I would have a chance to settle up with you, Jeff--but I'm not a giantslayer,

and anyway, you're no giant. There are a lot of people holding bullets with your name on them, but not
me--I think we're too alike for me to stay angry
with you.

Would it have been so hard to build a cool and
quirky bookstore instead of a soulless virtual
megamall? You were afraid:afraid to define the company, afraid the stock would drop, afraid not to
feed the monster. What you sacrifice reveals what
you value, and you're a fool if you think the world
will forgive you in the end.

Blah blah blah. I know you don't care what I say or
what the press says or even the evidence of your
own senses. You're sleeping well at night--you've
said so in interviews, and I'm certain it's true.
You're very busy tending the monster, keeping it
agile enough to outrun a million investors with
their long knives. Your own little version of
LOGAN'S RUN. Good luck with that.

As for me, I think I've safely ruined any chances
that I'll be returning to the corporate world:why
burn your bridges when you can nuke the entire
river? I said goodbye to health care, paychecks, and
social respect over the last year. I think it was
because I was afraid I was turning into you.

When I told people I'd be talking about you onstage
they always said they wanted to hear a "Jeff Bezos

laughing" impersonation. I would never do that, and it took me a long time to understand why. You are a genuinely happy and delighted person, the very best in all of us, like a brilliant, brilliant child. But your laugh terrifies me because even with these gifts you don't understand what you've done.

God, oh God, I hope you are forgiven.

md

16

Field Trip

And that's where this story should have ended but didn't. Our lives aren't stories: apart from birth and death they roll forward without natural beginnings or endings, and our own opening and closing are outside our ability to know or tell. We're left to define the ages of our lives by the events that carry weight for us—and by whatever makes sense.

Nothing about Amazon made sense for me: it was a fever I had passed through. After I got back from Spain I sat down to determine what I would be doing from then on. Money was going to get tight soon and I was getting married in just a few short months. They say God moves in mysterious ways, but He can also be frighteningly blunt. It was exactly then, in the midst of pedestrian apprehension, that I had my first vision while stinking drunk.

Let me clarify a few points: first, by "vision" I mean a numinous event that transcends both time and space, a singular moment of clarity. I've done my share of shrooms, acid, and ecstasy, but I have never experienced any sort of "vision"—I was always the guy who took the psychotropic drugs and felt exactly the same all night, then woke up in the morning to find my arms covered with burns from having acted on the belief that hot wax could indoctrinate me into The Cult of Pain, a shadowy delusional secret organization of my own making. Not especially visionary, considering the quantity and quality of drugs I used, which is why I now stick to alcohol.

Let's also be clear about what I mean by "stinking drunk." By this I mean *the drunk which stinks;* a smelly, nasty drunk; a full-blown trashy and hopeless drunk. This is not generic frat-boy-done-gone-had-a-lot-of-beer drunk, and this is not a schizoid Hunter-S.-Thompson-on-an-ether-binge-oh-my-God-the-walls-are-alligators drunk. You think ether and absinthe is cruel? Try a red-wine-and-fried-food drunk—fried chicken, white gravy, and Merlot. Chances are good your arteries won't even hold themselves open till dawn. It's a really, really slow Russian roulette.

Against the odds it was six A.M. and my posse was still drinking. The night before is a blur: I had given a performance, there had been some celebrating, some bar hopping, and finally we had grounded ourselves at the Cadillac Grill. It's a tawdry establishment: half greasy spoon, half gay bar, the only place I know of where you can get a plate of giant sausages, a gin and tonic, and a transvestite in your lap at the same time—damn close to heaven.

After a certain point the drinking began getting masochistic—no one wanted to go to bed, everyone kept pushing forward, hoping to break through the sound barrier of drinking, to the point where you get so poisoned that you dodge the inevitable hangover that is already bulging its way through your skull. Maybe we were trying to drink ourselves into readiness for our rendezvous; maybe we could feel that something weird was on the horizon.

You see, I've decided to go back to Amazon on this morning, to see Jeff and all the rest, to say goodbye—and the rule is that anyone who is as drunk as I am can come along. That still-valid ID has been burning a hole in my pocket for months, and this Sunday is a special day at Amazon World Headquarters.

It's my first time back since I walked out, and the Fortress continues to loom on the hill as if waiting for me. Security isn't a problem—I sign everyone else in as my guests. We follow all that exposed ductwork growing like kudzu up and up and up to arrive on the eighth floor, the huge central conference room with its gigantic panes of fifteen-foot-high glass and its breathtaking view of Seattle: pure dot-com hubris. You can stand on a stage backlit by Seattle, press the hidden control, and a screen comes down, the projector lights up . . . and you can show your plans for world conquest, or stock price valuations, or whatever it is you feel like demonstrating that day in the high holy colors of PowerPoint pie-chart glory. I'd seen Jeff do some of his best work here, and I had come here when no one was using it to stand up on the stage and pretend, for just a moment, to be Lex Luthor.

But nobody's making presentations today—we're all just

stumbling around because it's before eight A.M. on a Sunday, when even the most aggressive workaholics are at home. My group is deeply hung over and drunk at the same time, which is making dealing with spatial relationships difficult: I keep putting my bag down, forgetting I have put the bag down, checking my body for the bag, and discovering it's still on my body, all in one instant, like a mime who's been sucking on the crack pipe too long.

In order to keep a low profile and avoid making too much of a scene we keep going back to tables filled with corporate largesse: bagels and soda and soda and bagels and tiny, tiny cans of juice. I drink three eight-ounce cans of Ocean Spray CranGrape and drunkenly stuff two more in my pockets for later. I love the Ocean Spray CranGrape eight-ounce cans because I can drink so many of them at a sitting—I feel like I am a gigantic man, very powerful.

My friend John has taken too many bagels and people are looking at him funny. I'd help him out, explain to him that you need to look relaxed as you steal people's food or they'll know you don't belong, but I'm having my own problems—my mime act has attracted the attention of two or three former coworkers, who stop to say hello. We exchange pleasantries, and eventually they point at my badge, cock their heads, and say, "I heard you were . . . ?" to which I wave my arms in the air and blow air out of my nose while saying, "Weeell, you know . . ." So far that is keeping my cover secure, but my drinking-induced paranoia is making it hard to keep it together. I check for my bag again and eat another bagel.

I don't know where these bagels and sodas come from. I've heard legends that there are factories in the basements of every tech company where the slave-temps or morlocks bake fat bagels and send them up through pneumatic tubes to each conference room and meeting place in which their lords and masters wish to nosh. But it's not as though anyone really cares where they are from, so long as they're there for us to eat. And we're eating them, we're eating them, intently claiming our corporate freebie benefits, especially those of us for whom it is dorkishly illicit, and we don't really care because it's now seven-thirty A.M. on a Sunday.

But the children care a great deal. The employees' children who have been brought today for the Special Event care because they've now been fed on pure cane-sugar soda water for more than two hours. That shit is corn syrup that has been so finely refined that they might as well be mainlining sucrose—they're really amped up. They're wired, castrated little Winnie-the-Poohs; they're climbing right up the walls in *Matrix* outtakes. They hyperventilate and pass out like dogs that don't know any better.

My sweet fiancée turns to me, saying, "If even one goddamn rat-bastard little-shit kid gets in my way I'm going to snap his fucking neck!"—and that's when I know that we're too drunk to be here, because Jean-Michele, while frequently vulgar, is very rarely violent.

I am beginning to regret my impulsiveness. I have returned to the scene of the crime this morning for the Special Event: to watch the old Kingdome implode as we stand on the Fortress of Solitude's observation deck, enjoying the best view in the city.

If you're not familiar with the Kingdome stadium, it lurked at the southern end of Seattle, a nondescript concrete dome that housed baseball games and monster truck extravaganzas. It was ugly but functional, and we were there that morning to watch it be destroyed before it was paid for. The baseball teams and the corporations wanted a new stadium. The voters vetoed buying a new stadium in a referendum, but Paul Allen, one of the Northwest's patron Microsoft saints with buckets of fuck-you money, built one anyway and somehow the public ended up paying for most of it. The new one is much larger, built right next to where the old one's corpse would be, and is composed entirely of green plate glass, thin silver wires, and exposed ductwork—a shrine to the clean, modern era of high-tech, dot-com affluence.

Maybe everything would have turned out differently that morning if not for the terrifying snakeskin nostril lady, who comes up in her microminiskirt and her tighty-tight top, talking far too quickly. She's not wearing makeup to make herself attractive—she just wants to accentuate each and every one of her features in turn, so first she has these *huge* anime eyes, and then this gigantic pie-hole mouth, and then the nostrils—I could fit my fist inside these nostrils, they're just immense.

She's talking to my group and that's freaking me out a little, because everyone else keeps looking over to where she is and I feel certain at any moment that Employee #5 or Catch or one of the Codys is going to call my bluff. Everyone looks over to where she is because a pimply-faced adolescent is following her around with a TV camera, and I think it would be very *I Love Lucy* if one of my former coworkers sees me on their TV at home, talks to security, and I get hauled off for trespassing. So I'm trying to duck and weave away from the lens without looking as if that's what I'm doing, which is actually calling more attention to myself, which is actually my bigger problem. Jean-Michele holds my arm and hisses at me, "Calm the fuck down—you look like a dancing robot."

So I try to make nice and have a conversation with the swollen-faced strumpet but she's fading in and out so much that I can't resolve her looming features clearly, a sign I take to mean I may have been drinking too much, and I think she's saying, "Do you wanna dance? We need people to dance! Dance! Dance!" That request is so at odds with the reality of this room and my own altered state that I just stare back at her and twitch, which is making her repeat herself again and again, trying to get through. I keep thinking, *Man, this chick is dumb*, while she is clearly thinking, *Man, this big twitchy bastard is a fucking dork*. We are both right.

She is a second-string anchor for a local Fox affiliate that specializes in hairspray bulletins and consumer alerts about the secret perils of milk pasteurization. She is there to catch some footage of techies boogying down, celebrating their dot-com dominance by dancing to the fabulous music of Hit Explosion!, Seattle's worst cover band.

If you're not familiar with the work of Hit Explosion!, don't worry, you will be. On the day you die, Hit Explosion! will be piped into the express elevator to Hell, all the way to the bottom, where Casey Kasem will serenade you with stories of the orphaned Botswanan children to which each and every song in Hell is dedicated.

They're pretty by-the-numbers for the worst cover band you'll ever hear—there's a lot of dedication to tuning and posturing, and it seems that every member of the band has a different wig for every song. The weird thing is that the band isn't even playing whole songs—they're just playing *pieces* of songs. They get through the first few words of the chorus to "Celebrate" by Kool and the Gang and then stop short, pause, and then start over. "CELEBRA—! CELEB—! CELE—! CELEBRA—! CELEBRATE GOOD—! CELE—!" It's musical Chinese water torture. I think maybe my hearing is cutting out, the same way my vision did with the Nostril Lady—Kool and his Gang having some sort of sick revenge.

Then I turn and behold the most amazing tableau. The terrifying Nostril Lady has found some poor bastards and convinced them to dance. They're stumbling and shaking—most are geeks, and geeks are poor dancers at the best of times, and eight A.M. on a Sunday is surely the worst time to be dancing. They stagger like wounded dinosaurs from one foot to another, swaying in a lame mockery of all things with rhythm. The Nostril Lady's assistant has to join the group and fake it up into something that looks believable.

As soon as she gets them dancing she cues the band, they start, "CE—LEBRATE!" She cues the camera, gets right in front of it, hot TV light flooding her as she says, "At Amazon.com they're 'getting jiggy with it' all over Earth's Largest Store! Check out these excited people here for the end of the Kingdome and the beginning of a new era in Seattle—don't you all wish you were here?" At this she cues the group and a ragged cry goes up, kind of like real people cheering but at the end of a long tunnel.

And then it all ends at once—she gives the signal, they turn off the camera, the band stops playing, the people who've been dancing wander away in search of bagels. Today's media event is over. To us it is sad and forced, but it plays well for the public and within the picture tubes and browser windows tuning in it will be *on message,* telling the same story we've always wanted told, the only story that the media and the company would ever allow, the story I swallowed and spit up and helped to forge, the myth I would have imparted to my sleeping children. I'm left there thinking, *Did this just happen or was this a metaphor?*

I stand there among my former coworkers and I want to hate them so completely that I could kill with a look. Hating them would prove that I have changed, that I have left this life behind. But I don't feel that way. I just feel lonely—and I miss them, I miss all of them as I stand in their midst, trying to overhear every conversation about what is coming next, what Jeff will do, what we'll all be doing together. I'm a ghost in this house, an outsider, and it horrifies me. I suddenly want security to find me and take me and taser me against these windows, humiliate me, brand me a freak and an outsider, free me.

When you leave a place, you like to think that things will change, not just for you but for the people you leave behind. You're gone and they'll feel your absence. They'll remember you for what you did, the way you licked the envelopes, the way you were the only one who made that fax machine work. Everyone will talk about how it will never be the same. But we all know that that's not the way it works. In the end it is simple: you left and they stayed. When you go you're always the one that's left behind.

▶ So we crowd together on the balcony as the minutes and then seconds tick down. The cameras focus on the doomed stadium and not the tech intelligentsia now, the band has packed up its wigs and hit the road, the children are still bouncing around the room like stray bullets, and we are watching. We've eaten the bagels. We're waiting for the show to begin.

Someone starts counting and at once we all join together, the common voice of the spectacle, like New Year's when the ball is dropping, and we count: nine, eight, seven—and all of us—six, five, four—and we're all doing it—three, two, one— and we all say zero together, which is really weird; I've never heard people do that before. *Zero*, a single declaration of the absolute negative.

Far below us, the gigantic sports stadium has explosives professionally packed in deep holes drilled into its foundation, wired up along the massive girders and beams, snaking through all its innards like a decisive and terminal cancer. Across the city men and women and children watch, and on their televisions

Field Trip

every station switches between the views they have from the ground, from space, from helicopters, from remote cameras inside the dome waiting to capture the sky falling in, from high-end infrared cameras that will collect the tracery of detonations and paint them in false color so that we can rewind and watch the collapse forward and backward and forward again. How long have we waited for this? How long have we longed to kill off this ugly concrete dome, wipe out this piece of untelegenic and pedestrian history so that something as worthy as this new stadium, the most expensive on the planet, can rise? It hulks next to its soon-to-be-executed brother, costing more in interest every day than most of us will make in a lifetime, the latest, greatest, coolest thing of this moment.

And nothing happens. All over Seattle our breath is caught in our throats and we're craning our necks like ostriches, as though the extra inch in height will reveal something the moment the cataclysm starts. Each and every ostrich-necked person is staring down at the not-exploding building and the silence is absolute. Something is going wrong with the script.

And this is it. This is the moment of my vision, the moment I've waited for my whole life. It's not the way I wanted it to be—no one would want it to be this way—but we play the hands we're dealt. In this one moment we are all looking at this one point, staring down at this edifice and wishing, praying recklessly: let it do something. Please. Let it do anything at all, we don't care, please, we got up so early this morning, we've been on this ride for so long, please. Let it collapse to the ground, let it implode, let it explode, let it fly up into the air, we don't care, just do something, anything, please, break our happiness apart and let us be lifted up in pieces. You can't leave us here—don't suspend us in this moment, hanging at the top of the precipice. We've been on this ride for so long, we need a little resolution.

In the silence I'm frightened of us, standing up above this city, and frightened for us. I find myself thinking of all the logging towns in my home state of Maine, and how the day the company pulls out those towns are dead towns and the people in them dead people: they don't know it yet, but they'll learn. Can it happen in reverse? Can you pour so much prosperity into a place or a time that it flows into every orifice and the people and place itself forget who they are, forget their own names?

This is the zero hour from which I can mark a new calendar: a few seconds from now the dome will flash as the sequence begins, the charges unfold one after another like bright soldiers, and the whole structure blossoms as an ugly flower and then falls into simple debris. A few weeks from now it is April and the NASDAQ is bursting into flames and plunging out of the sky as companies begin to choke and struggle, never built for winter. A few months further and I am standing at the altar in Saint Joseph's watching my bride walk toward me on the exact anniversary of my hire: had I chosen to stay at Amazon I would have even more options worth cold cash this day, options whose actual value was burning down to less than zero moment by moment. Now it is a year further, and layoffs are vaporizing the careers of almost everyone I ever worked with, the company dropping them on a moment's notice after years of selfless service that wasn't entirely selfless. Amazon is praying for Wal-Mart to save it, the pundits are shaking their heads at Amazon's spin and shrugging like they never bought into it, laughing at the company as it struggles, desperate and defiant and bleeding millions, determined to win at any cost a prize long gone. Now it is that terrible September and other buildings are falling. I am in New York and I watch them fall and it is the difference between the idea of the knife and being stabbed—and at that

Field Trip

moment this era becomes immediately historical, it cannibalizes itself, closing up after long illness because the money is gone, the idealism is gone, and finally, now, the naïveté is gone. We won't see those days again. We're left with a series of snapshots: now Jeff on the cover of *Time,* now in a Taco Bell ad, now nowhere—instant kitsch, a bygone era that came and went so fast it didn't even say goodbye.

That is the future speaking, but I only know this moment, looking down to where the explosion will happen. Next to me is the woman who will become my wife, standing so close I can feel the breath pent up inside her. I'm holding her hand and between our two palms is a sentence like a pebble I am holding on to and that sentence is: I will never work again the way I worked here. I am making this promise again and again, I make it every night, and I'm still standing, waiting to see what happens next.

↑ ↑ ↑

Acknowledgments

Some facts were injured in the telling of this story. The truth, however, remains unharmed.

Debts are owed to John Tynes, Dennis Gilbert, Daniel Greenberg, the late Speakeasy Backroom, the lovely shop Shakespeare's Sister on Court Street in Brooklyn where the majority of this book was written, and to LeRoy and Virginia Bowen in whose home this book was rewritten and revised.

I will never be able to adequately thank Rachel Klayman, my editor. Her warmth, care, and diamond-hard wit were invaluable—she so tirelessly strove to elevate and sharpen my prose that I learned a huge amount through her notes, her measured praise, and her uncomfortable silence when I missed. She is one of the finest teachers I have ever had.

The material within this book originated as a one-man show of the same name. *21 Dog Years* received its first public performance on February 11, 2001, at the Speakeasy Backroom in Seattle. It subsequently opened Off Broadway at the Cherry Lane Theatre on May 9, 2002. Both productions were directed by Jean-Michele Gregory, who remains my constant collaborator and sparring partner.

About the Author

Mike Daisey's one-man show includes *21 Dog Years, Wasting Your Breath,* and *I Miss the Cold War.* They have been performed in unheated garages, hotel ballrooms, unused hallways, and Off Broadway. He has worked as a security officer, web pornsniffer, high school teacher, blood plasma seller, archivist, telemarketer, roofer, cow innard remover, law firm receptionist, cold caller, rape counselor, DJ, freelance writer, accountant, night janitor in a home for the violently mentally ill, and dot-com wage slave. He lives in Brooklyn, and may be found on the web at mikedaisey.com.

Printed in the United States
82463LV00002B/236